AN

APOLOGY

FOR

The Bible,

IN

A SERIES OF LETTERS

ADDRESSED TO

THOMAS PAINE,

*Author of a Book entitled " The AGE of REASON,"
part the Second, being an Investigation of
True and Fabulous Theology.*

BY THE LATE

RICHARD WATSON, D.D.

LORD BISHOP OF LANDAFF, AND REGIUS PROFESSOR OF DIVINITY
IN THE UNIVERSITY OF CAMBRIDGE.

CAMBRIDGE:

Printed by J. Smith, Printer to the University;

And Sold by *F. C. & J. Rivington*, St. Paul's Church-yard; *J. Mawman*,
30 Ludgate Street, London; and *J. Deighton & Sons*, Cambridge.

1820

Price Eight Pence.

CAMBRIDGE UNIVERSITY PRESS
Cambridge, New York, Melbourne, Madrid, Cape Town,
Singapore, São Paulo, Delhi, Tokyo, Mexico City

Cambridge University Press
The Edinburgh Building, Cambridge CB2 8RU, UK

Published in the United States of America by
Cambridge University Press, New York

www.cambridge.org
Information on this title: www.cambridge.org/9781107600041

© Cambridge University Press 1820

First published 1820
First paperback edition 2011

A catalogue record for this publication is available from the British Library

ISBN 978-1-107-60004-1 Paperback

LETTER I.

SIR,

I HAVE lately met with a book of yours, entitled——
"THE AGE OF REASON, part the second, being an investigation of true and fabulous theology;"——and I think it
not inconsistent with my station, and the duty I owe to
society, to trouble you and the world with some observa-
tions on so extraordinary a performance. Extraordinary
I esteem it; not from any novelty in the objections which
you have produced against revealed religion, (for I find
little or no novelty in them,) but from the zeal with which
you labour to disseminate your opinions, and from the
confidence with which you esteem them true. You perceive, by this, that I give you credit for your sincerity,
how much soever I may question your wisdom, in writing
in such a manner on such a subject: and I have no reluctance in acknowledging that you possess a considerable
share of energy of language, and acuteness of investigation;
though I must be allowed to lament, that these talents
have not been applied in a manner more useful to human
kind, and more creditable to yourself.

I begin with your preface. You therein state——that
you had long had an intention of publishing your thoughts
upon religion, but that you had originally reserved it to
a later period in life.-——I hope there is no want of charity
in saying, that it would have been fortunate for the chris-
tian world, had your life been terminated before you had
fulfilled your intention. In accomplishing your purpose
you will have unsettled the faith of thousands; rooted
from the minds of the unhappy virtuous all their comfort-

A

able affurance of future recompence; have annihilated in
the minds of the flagitious all their fears of future punifhment; you will have given the reins to the domination of
every paffion, and have thereby contributed to the intro-
duction of the public infecurity, and of the private un-
happinefs, ufually and almoft neceffarily accompanying a
ftate of corrupted morals.

No one can think worfe of confeffion to a prieft and
fubfequent abfolution, as practifed in the church of Rome,
than I do; but I cannot, with you, attribute the guillotine-
maffacres to that caufe. Men's minds were not prepared,
as you fuppofe, for the commiffion of all manner of crimes,
by any doctrines of the church of Rome, corrupted as
I efteem it, but by their not thoroughly believing even
that religion. What may not fociety expect from thofe
who fhall imbibe the principles of your book?

A fever, which you and thofe about you expected
would prove mortal, made you remember, with renewed
fatisfaction, that you had written the former part of your
Age of Reafon—and you know therefore, you fay, by
experience, the confcientious trial of your own principles.
I admit this declaration to be a proof of the fincerity of
your perfuafion, but I cannot admit it to be any proof of
the truth of your principles. What is confcience? Is it,
as has been thought, an internal monitor implanted in us
by the Supreme Being, and dictating to us on all occafions,
what is right or wrong? Or is it merely our own judgment of the moral rectitude or turpitude of our own
actions? I take the word (with Mr. Locke) in the latter,
as in the only intelligible fenfe. Now who fees not that
our judgments of virtue and vice, right and wrong, are
not always formed from an enlightened and difpaffionate
ufe of our reafon, in the inveftigation of truth? They are
more generally formed from the nature of the religion we
profefs; from the quality of the civil government under
which we live; from the general manners of the age, or
the particular manners of the perfons with whom we
affociate; from the education we have had in our youth;
from the books we have read at a more advanced period;

and from other accidental caufes. Who fees not that, on this account, confcience may be conformable or repugnant to the law of nature?——may be certain, or doubtful?—— and that it can be no criterion of moral rectitude, even when it is certain, becaufe the certainty of an opinion is no proof of its being a right opinion? A man may be certainly perfuaded of an error in reafoning, or of an untruth in matters of fact. It is a maxim of every law, human and divine, that a man ought never to act in oppofition to his confcience; but it will not from thence follow, that he will, in obeying the dictates of his confcience, on all occafions act right. An inquifitor who burns Jews and hereticks: a Robefpierre, who maffacres innocent and harmlefs women; a robber, who thinks that all things ought to be in common, and that a ftate of property is an unjuft infringement of natural liberty;——thefe, and a thoufand perpetrators of different crimes, may all follow the dictates of confcience; and may, at the real or fuppofed approach of death, remember "with renewed fatisfaction," the worft of their tranfactions, and experience, without difmay, "a confcientious trial of their principles." But this their confcientious compofure can be no proof to others of the rectitude of their principles, and ought to be no pledge to themfelves of their innocence, in adhering to them.

I have thought fit to make this remark, with a view of fuggefting to you a confideration of great importance ——whether you have examined calmly, and according to the beft of your ability, the arguments by which the truth of revealed religion may, in the judgment of learned and impartial men, be eftablifhed?——You will allow, that thoufands of learned and impartial men, (I fpeak not of priefts, who, however, are, I truft, as learned and impartial as yourfelf, but of laymen of the moft fplendid talents,)——you will allow that thoufands of thefe, in all ages, have embraced revealed religion as true. Whether thefe men have all been in an error, enveloped in the darknefs of ignorance, fhackled by the chains of fuperftition, whilft you and a few others have enjoyed light and liberty, is a queſtion I ſubmit to the deciſion of your readers.

If you have made the beſt examination you can, and yet reject revealed religion as an impoſture, I pray that God may pardon what I eſteem your error. And whether you have made this examination or not, does not become me or any man to determine. That Goſpel, which you deſpiſe, has taught me this moderation; it has ſaid to me ——"Who art thou that judgeſt another man's ſervant? To his own maſter he ſtandeth or falleth."——I think that you are in an error; but whether that error be to you a vincible or an invincible error, I preſume not to determine. I know indeed where it is ſaid——"that the preaching of the croſs is to them that periſh fooliſhneſs,——and that if the goſpel be hid, it is hid to them that are loſt." The conſequence of your unbelief muſt be left to the juſt and merciful judgment of Him, who alone knoweth the mechaniſm and the liberty of our underſtandings; the origin of our opinions; the ſtrength of our prejudices; the excellencies and defects of our reaſoning faculties.

I ſhall, deſignedly, write this and the following letters in a popular manner; hoping that thereby they may ſtand a chance of being peruſed by that claſs of readers, for whom your work ſeems to be particularly calculated, and who are the moſt likely to be injured by it. The really learned are in no danger of being infected by the poiſon of infidelity: they will excuſe me, therefore, for having entered, as little as poſſible, into deep diſquiſitions concerning the authenticity of the Bible. The ſubject has been ſo learnedly, and ſo frequently handled by other writers, that it does not want (I had almoſt ſaid, it does not admit) any farther proof. And it is the more neceſſary to adopt this mode of anſwering your book, becauſe you diſclaim all learned appeals to other books, and undertake to prove, from the Bible itſelf, that it is unworthy of credit. I hope to ſhew, from the Bible itſelf, the direct contrary. But in caſe any of your readers ſhould think that you had not put forth all your ſtrength, by not referring for proof of your opinion to ancient authors; left they fhould fufpect that all ancient authors are in your favour; I will venture to affirm, that had you made a learned appeal to all the ancient books in the world, facred or profane, Chriftian, Jewifh, or Pagan, inftead of leffening, they would have eftablifhed, the credit and authority of the Bible as the Word of God.

Quitting your preface, let us proceed to the work it-felf; in which there is much repetition, and a defect of proper arrangement. I will follow your tract, however, as nearly as I can. The firft queftion you propofe for con-fideration is——" Whether there is fufficient authority for believing the Bible to be the Word of God, or whether there is not?"—You determine this queftion in the negative, upon what you are pleafed to call moral evidence. You hold it impoffible that the Bible can be the Word of God, becaufe it is therein faid, that the Ifraelites deftroyed the Canaanites by the exprefs command of God: and to be-lieve the Bible to be true, we muft, you affirm, unbelieve all our belief of the moral juftice of God; for wherein, you afk, could crying or fmiling infants offend?——I am afto-nifhed that fo acute a reafoner fhould attempt to difparage the Bible, by bringing forward this exploded and frequent-ly refuted objection of Morgan, Tindal, and Bolingbroke. You profefs yourfelf to be a deift, and to believe that there is a God, who created the univerfe, and eftablifhed the laws of nature, by which it is fuftained in exiftence. You profefs that from the contemplation of the works of God, you derive a knowledge of his attributes; and you reject the Bible, becaufe it afcribes to God things incon-fiftent (as you fuppofe) with the attributes which you have difcovered to belong to him; in particular, you think it repugnant to his moral juftice, that he fhould doom to deftruction the crying or fmiling infants of the Canaanites. —Why do you not maintain it to be repugnant to his mo-ral juftice, that he fhould fuffer crying or fmiling infants to be fwallowed up by an earthquake, drowned by an inun-dation, confumed by a fire, ftarved by a famine, or de-ftroyed by a peftilence? The Word of God is in perfect harmony with his work; crying or fmiling infants are fubjected to death in both. We believe that the earth, at the exprefs command of God, opened her mouth, and fwallowed up Korah, Dathan, and Abiram, with their wives, their fons, and their little ones. This you efteem fo repugnant to God's moral juftice, that you fpurn, as fpurious, the book in which the circumftance is related. When Catania, Lima, and Lifbon, were feverally deftroyed by earthquakes, men with their wives, their fons, and their little ones, were fwallowed up alive——why do you not fpurn, as fpurious, the book of nature, in which this fact is certainly written, and from the perufal of which you infer the moral juftice of God? You will, probably, reply, that the evils which the Canaanites fuffered from the exprefs command of God, were different from thofe which are brought on mankind by the operation of the laws of nature.——Different! in what?—Not in the magnitude of the evil—not in the fubjects of fufferance—not in the author of it—for my philofophy, at leaft, inftructs me to believe, that God not only primarily formed, but that he hath, through all ages, executed, the laws of nature; and that he will, through all eternity, adminifter them, for the general happinefs of his creatures, whether we can, on every occafion, difcern that end or not.

I am far from being guilty of the impiety of queftioning the exiftence of the moral juftice of God, as proved either by natural or revealed religion; what I contend for is fhortly this—that you have no right, in fairnefs of reafoning, to urge any apparent deviation from moral juftice, as an argument againft revealed religion, becaufe you do not urge an equally apparent deviation from it, as an argument againft natural religion: you reject the former, and admit the latter, without confidering that, as to your objection, they muft ftand or fall together.

As to the Canaanites, it is needlefs to enter into any proof of the depraved ftate of their morals; they were a wicked people in the time of Abraham, and they, even then, were devoted to deftruction by God; but their iniquity was not then full. In the time of Mofes, they were idolaters, facrificers of their own crying or fmiling infants; devourers of human flefh; addicted to unnatural luft; immerfed in the filthinefs of all manner of vice. Now, I think, it will be impoffible to prove, that it was a proceeding contrary to God's moral juftice to exterminate fo wicked a people. He made the Ifraelites the executors of his vengeance; and in doing this, he gave fuch an evident and terrible proof of his abomination of vice, as could not fail to ftrike the furrounding nations with aftonifhment and terror, and to imprefs on the minds of the Ifraelites, what they were to expect, if they followed the example of the nations whom he commanded them to cut off. "Ye fhall not commit any of thefe abominations——that the land fpew not you out alfo, as it fpewed out the nations that were before you." How ftrong and defcriptive this language! the vices of the inhabitants were fo abominable, that the very land was fick of them, and forced vomit them forth, as the ftomach difgorges a deadly poifon.

I have often wondered what could be the reafon that men, not deftitute of talents, fhould be defirous of undermining the authority of revealed religion, and ftudious in expofing, with a malignant and illiberal exultation, every little difficulty attending the Scriptures, to popular animadverfion and contempt. I am not willing to attribute this ftrange propenfity to what Plato attributed the atheifm of his time——to profligacy of. manners——to affectation of fingularity——to grofs ignorance, affuming the femblance of deep refearch and fuperior fagacity;——I had rather refer it to an impropriety of judgment, refpecting the manners, and mental acquirements, of human kind in the firft ages of the world. Moft unbelievers argue as if they thought that man, in remote and rude antiquity, in the very birth and infancy of our fpecies, had the fame diftinct conceptions of one, eternal, invifible, incorporeal, infinitely wife, powerful, and good God, which they themfelves have now. This I look upon as a great miftake, and a pregnant fource of infidelity. Human kind, by a long experience; by the inftitutions of civil fociety; by the cultivation of arts and fciences; by, as I believe, divine inftruction actually given

to fome, and traditionally communicated to all; is in a far
more diftinguifhed fituation, as to the powers of the mind,
than it was in the childhood of the world. The hiftory of
man, is the hiftory of the providence of God; who, willing the fupreme felicity of all his creatures, has adapted
his government to the capacity of those, who in different
ages were the fubjects of it. The hiftory of any one nation
throughout all ages, and that of all nations in the fame age,
are but feparate parts of one great plan, which God is car-
rying on for the moral melioration of mankind. But who
can comprehend the whole of this immenfe defign? The
fhortnefs of life, the weaknefs of our faculties, the inade-
quacy of our means of information, confpire to make it
impoffible for us, worms of the earth! infects of an hour!
completely to underftand any one of its parts. No man,
who well weighs the fubject, ought to be furprifed, that in
the hiftories of ancient times many things fhould occur
foreign to our manners, the propriety and neceffity of
which we cannot clearly apprehend.

It appears incredible to many, that God Almighty
fhould have had colloquial intercourfe with our firft
parents; that he fhould have contracted a kind of friend-
fhip for the patriarchs, and entered into covenants with
them; that he fhould have fufpended the laws of nature in
Egypt; fhould have been fo apparently partial as to become
the God and governor of one particular nation; and fhould
have fo far demeaned himfelf as to give to that people a
burthenfome ritual of worfhip, ftatutes and ordinances,
many of which feem to be beneath the dignity of his attention, unimportant and impolitic. I have converfed with
many deifts, and have always found that the ftrangenefs of
thefe things was the only reafon for their difbelief of them:
nothing fimilar has happened in their time; they will not,
therefore, admit, that thefe events have really taken place
at any time. As well might a child, when arrived at a
ftate of manhood, contend that he had never either ftood
in need or experienced the foftering care of a mother's
kindnefs, the wearifome attention of his nurfe, or the inftruction and difcipline of his fchoolmafter. The Supreme

Being felected one family from an idolatrous world; nurfed
it up, by various acts of his providence, into a great nation; communicated to that nation a knowledge of his holinefs, juftice, mercy, power, and wifdom; difteminated
them at various times, through every part of the earth,
that they might be a "leaven to leaven the whole lump,"
that they might affure all other nations of the exiftence of
one fupreme God, the creator and preferver of the world,
the only proper object of adoration. With what reafon
can we expect, that what was done to one nation, not out
of any partiality to them, but for the general good, fhould
be done to all? that the mode of inftruction, which was
fuited to the infancy of the world, fhould be extended to
the maturity of its manhood, or to the imbecility of its
old age? I own to you, that when I confider how nearly
man, in a favage ftate, approaches to the brute creation,
as to intellectual excellence; and when I contemplate his
miferable attainments as to the knowledge of God, in a
civilized ftate, when he has had no divine inftruction on
the fubject, or when that inftruction has been forgotten,
(for all men have known fomething of God from tradition,) I cannot but admire the wifdom and goodnefs of the
Supreme Being, in having let himfelf down to our appre-
henfions; in having given to mankind, in the earlieft ages,
fenfible and extraordinary proofs of his exiftence and attributes; in having made the Jewifh and Chriftian difpenfations mediums to convey to all men, through all ages, that
knowledge concerning himfelf, which he had vouchfafed
to give immediately to the firft. I own it is ftrange, very
ftrange, that he fhould have made an immediate manifeftation of himfelf in the firft ages of the world; but what is
there that is not ftrange? It is ftrange that you and I are
here——that there is water, and earth, and air, and fire——
that there is a fun, and moon, and ftars——that there is generation, corruption, reproduction. I can account ulti-
mately for none of thefe things, without recurring to him
who made every thing. I alfo am his workmanfhip, and
look up to him with hope of prefervation through all eternity; I adore him for his word as well as for his work; his

work I cannot comprehend, but his word hath affured me
of all that I am concerned to know——that he hath prepared everlafting happinefs for thofe who love and obey
him. This you will call preachment:——I will have done
with it; but the fubject is fo vaft, and the plan of Providence, in my opinion, fo obvioufly wife and good, that I
can never think of it without having my mind filled with
piety, admiration, and gratitude.

In addition to the moral evidence (as you are pleafed
to think it) againft the Bible, you threaten in the progrefs
of your work, to produce fuch other evidence as even a
prieft cannot deny. A philofopher in fearch of truth for-
feits with me all claim to candour and impartiality, when
he introduces railing for reafoning, vulgar and illiberal
farcafms in the room of argument. I will not imitate the
example you fet me: but examine what you fhall produce,
with as much coolnefs and refpect, as if you had given the
priefts no provocation; as if you were a man of the moft
unblemifhed character, fubject to no prejudices, actuated
by no bad defigns, not liable to have abufe retorted upon
you with fuccefs.

LETTER II.

Before you commence your grand attack upon the
Bible, you wifh to eftablifh a difference between the evidence neceffary to prove the authenticity of the Bible, and
that of any other ancient book. I am not furprifed at
your anxiety on this head; for all writers on the fubject
have agreed in thinking that St. Auftin reafoned well,
when, in vindicating the genuinenefs of the Bible, he afked——
"What proofs have we that the works of Plato, Ariftotle,
Cicero, Varro, and other profane authors, were written by
thofe whofe names they bear; unlefs it be that this has
been an opinion generally received at all times, and by all

thofe who have lived fince thefe authors?" This writer was convinced, that the evidence which eftablifhed the genuinenefs of any profane book would eftablifh that of a facred book, and I profefs myfelf to be of the fame opinion, notwithftanding what you have advanced to the contrary.

In this part your ideas feem to me to be confufed; I do not fay that you, defignedly, jumble together mathematical fcience and hiftorical evidence; the knowledge acquired by demonftration, and the probability derived from teftimony.——You know but of one ancient book, that authoritatively challenges univerfal confent and belief, and that is Euclid's Elements.——If I were difpofed to make frivolous objections, I fhould fay that even Euclid's Elements had not met with univerfal confent: that there had been men, both in ancient and modern times, who had queftioned the intuitive evidence of fome of his axioms, and denied the juftnefs of fome of his demonftrations: but, admitting the truth, I do not fee the pertinency of your obfervation. You are attempting to fubvert the authenticity of the Bible, and you tell us that Euclid's Elements are certainly true.——What then? Does it follow that the Bible is certainly falfe? the moft illiterate fcrivener in the kingdom does not want to be informed, that the examples in his Wingate's Arithmetic, are proved by a different kind of reafoning from that by which he perfuades himfelf to believe, that there was fuch a perfon as Henry VIII. or that there is fuch a city as Paris.

It may be of ufe to remove this confufion in your argument to ftate, diftinctly, the difference between the genuinenefs, and the authenticity, of a book. A genuine book, is that which was written by the perfon whofe name it bears as the author of it. An authentic book, is that which relates matters of fact, as they really happened. A book may be genuine without being authentic; and a book may be authentic without being genuine. The books written by Richardfon and Fielding are genuine books, though the hiftories of Clariffa and Tom Jones are fables. The hiftory of the ifland of Formofa is a genuine book; it was written by Pfalmanazar: but it is not an authentic book, (though it was long efteemed as fuch, and tranflated into different languages,) for the author, in the latter part of his life took fhame to himfelf for having impofed on the world, and confeffed it was a mere romance. Anfon's Voyage may be confidered as an authentic book, it, pro- bably, containing a true narration of the principal events recorded in it; but it is not a genuine book, having not been written by Walter, to whom it is afcribed, but by Robins.

This diftinction between the genuinenefs and authen- ticity of a book, will affift us in detecting the fallacy of an argument, which you ftate with great confidence in the part of your work now under confideration, and which you frequently allude to, in other parts, as conclufive evi- dence againft the truth of the Bible. Your argument ftands thus——If it be found that the books afcribed to Mofes, Jofhua and Samuel, were not written by Mofes, Jofhua, and Samuel, every part of the authority and au- thenticity of thefe books is gone at once. —I prefume to think otherwife. The genuinenefs of thefe books (in the judgment of thofe who fay that they were written by thefe authors) will certainly be gone; but their authen- ticity may remain; they may ftill contain a true account of real tranfactions, though the names of the writers of them fhould be found to be different from what they are generally efteemed to be.

Had, indeed, Mofes faid that he wrote the firft five books of the Bible; and had Jofhua and Samuel faid that they wrote the books which are refpectively attributed to them; and had it been found that Mofes, Jofhua, and Samuel, did not write thefe books; then, I grant, the au- thority of the whole would have been gone at once; thefe men would have been found liars, as to the genuinenefs of the books; and this proof of their want of veracity, in one point, would have invalidated their teftimony in every other; thefe books would have been juftly ftigmatized, as neither genuine nor authentic.

An hiftory may be true, though it fhould not only be afcribed to a wrong author, but though the author of it fhould not be known; anonymous teftimony does not deftroy the reality of facts, whether natural or miraculous. Had Lord Clarendon publifhed his Hiftory of the Rebellion, without prefixing his name to it; or had the hiftory of Titus Livius come down to us, under the name of Valerius Flaccus, or Valerius Maximus; the facts mentioned in thefe hiftories would have been equally certain.

As to your affertion, that the miracles recorded in Tacitus, and in other profane hiftorians, are quite as well authenticated as thofe of the Bible—it being a mere affertion deftitute of proof, may be properly anfwered by a contrary affertion. I take the liberty then to fay, that the evidence for the miracles recorded in the Bible, is, both in kind and degree, fo greatly fuperior to that for the prodigies mentioned by Livy, or the miracles related by Tacitus, as to juftify us in giving credit to the one as the work of God, and in withholding it from the other as the effect of fuperftition and impofture. This method of derogating from the credibility of Chriftianity, by oppofing to the miracles of our Saviour, the tricks of ancient impoftors, feems to have originated with Hierocles in the fourth century; and it has been adopted by unbelievers from that time to this; with this difference, indeed, that the heathens of the third and fourth century admitted that Jefus wrought miracles; but left that admiffion fhould have compelled them to abandon their gods and become Chriftians, they faid, that their *Apollonius,* their *Apuleius,* their *Arifteas,* did as great: whilft modern deifts deny the fact of Jefus having ever wrought a miracle. And they have fome reafon for this proceeding; they are fenfible that the gofpel miracles are fo different in all their circumftances, from thofe related in Pagan ftory, that if they admit them to have been performed, they muft admit Chriftianity to be true; hence they have fabricated a kind of deiftical axiom——that no human teftimony can eftablifh the credibility of a miracle.——This, though it has been an hundred times refuted, is ftill infifted upon, as if its truth had never been queftioned, and could not be difproved.

You " proceed to examine the authenticity of the

B

Bible; and you begin, you say, with what are called the five books of Mofes, Genefis, Exodus, Leviticus, Numbers, and Deuteronomy. Your intention, you profefs, is to fhew that thefe books are fpurious, and that Mofes is not the author of them; and ftill farther, that they were not written in the time of Mofes, nor till feveral hundred years afterwards; that they are no other than an attempted hiftory of the life of Mofes, and of the times in which he is faid to have lived, and alfo of the times prior thereto, written by fome very ignorant and ftupid pretender to authorfhip, feveral hundred years after the death of Mofes.''—In this paffage the utmoft force of your attack on the authority of the five books of Mofes is clearly ftated. You are not the firft who has ftarted this diffi- culty; it is a difficulty, indeed, of modern date; having not been heard of, either in the fynagogue, or out of it till the twelfth century. About that time *Eben Ezra,* a Jew of great erudition, noticed fome paffages (the fame that you have brought forward) in the five firft books of the Bible, which he thought had not been written by Mofes, but inferted by fome perfon after the death of Mofes. But he was far from maintaining as you do, that thefe books were written by fome ignorant and ftupid pretender to authorfhip, many hundred years after the death of Mofes. *Hobbes* contends that the books of Mofes are fo called, not from their having been written by Mofes, but from their containing an account of Mofes. *Spinoza* fupported the fame opinion; and *Le Clerc,* a very able theological critic of the laft and prefent century, once entertained the fame notion. You fee that this fancy has had fome patrons before you; the merit or the demerit, the fagacity or the temerity of having afferted, that Mofes is not the author of the Pentateuch, is not exclufively yours. *Le Clerc,* indeed, you muft not boaft of. When his judgment was matured by age, he was afhamed of what he had written on the fubject in his younger years; he made a public recantation of his error, by annexing to his commentary on Genefis, a Latin differtation——con- cerning Mofes, the author of the Pentateuch, and his defign in compofing it. If in your future life you fhould chance to change your opinion on the fubject, it will be an honour to your character to emulate the integrity, and to imitate the example, of *Le Clerc.* The Bible is not the only book which has undergone the fate of being reprobated as fpurious, after it had been received as genuine and authentic for many ages. It has been maintained that the hiftory of *Herodotus* was written in the time of *Conftantine;* and that the claffics are forgeries of the thirteenth or fourteenth century. Thefe extravagant reveries amufed the world at the time of their publication, and have long fince funk into oblivion. You efteem all prophets to be fuch lying rafcals, that I dare not venture to predict the fate of your book.

Before you produce your main objection to the genuinenefs of the books of Mofes, you affert—" That there is no affirmative evidence that Mofes is the author of them."—What? no affirmative evidence! In the eleventh century *Maimonides* drew up a confeffion of faith for the Jews, which all of them at this day admit; it confifts of only thirteen articles; and two of them have refpect to Mofes; one affirming the authenticity, the other the genuinenefs of his books.—The doctrine and prophecy of Mofes is true—The law that we have was given by Mofes. This is the faith of the Jews at prefent, and has been their faith ever fince the deftruction of their city and temple; it was their faith in the time when the authors of the New Teftament wrote; it was their faith during their captivity in Babylon; in the time of their kings and judges; and no period can be fhewn, from the age of Mofes to the prefent hour, in which it was not their faith.—Is this no affirmative evidence? I cannot defire a ftronger. *Jofephus*, in his book againft *Appion*, writes thus—" We have only two and twenty books which are to be believed as of divine authority, and which comprehend the hiftory of all ages; five belong to Mofes, which contain the original of man, and the tradition of the fucceffion of generations, down to his death, which takes in a compafs of about three thoufand years." Do you confider this as no affirmative evidence? Why fhould

I mention *Juvenal* fpeaking of the volume which Mofes had written ? Why enumerate a long lift of profane authors, all bearing teftimony to the fact of *Mofes* being the leader and the lawgiver of the Jewifh nation ? and if a lawgiver, furely a writer of the laws. But what fays the Bible? In Exodus it fays——" Mofes wrote all the words of the Lord, and took the book of the covenant, and read in the audience of the people."——In Deuteronomy it fays—— " And it came to pafs, when Mofes had made an end of writing the words of this law in a book, until they were finifhed, (this furely imports the finifhing a laborious work,) that Mofes commanded the Levites which bare the ark of the covenant of the Lord, faying, ' Take this book of the law, and put it in the fide of the ark of the cove- nant of the Lord your God, that it may be there for a witnefs againft thee.'" This is faid in Deuteronomy, which is a kind of repetition or abridgment of the four preceding books ; and it is well known that the Jews gave the name of the Law to the firft five books of the Old Teftament. What poffible doubt can there be that Mofes wrote the books in queftion ? I could accumulate many other paffages from the Scriptures to this purpofe ; but if what I have advanced will not convince you that there is affirmative evidence, and of the ftrongeft kind, for Mofes' being the author of thefe books, nothing that I can advance will convince you.

What if I fhould grant all you undertake to prove (the ftupidity and ignorance of the writer excepted ?——) What if I fhould admit, that *Samuel,* or *Ezra,* or fome other learned Jew, compofed thefe books, from public records, many years after the death of Mofes ! Will it follow, that there was no truth in them ? According to my logic, it will only follow, that they are not genuine books ; every fact recorded in them may be true, when- ever, or by whomfoever they were written. It cannot be faid that the Jews had no public records, the Bible fur- nifhes abundance of proof to the contrary. I by no means admit, that thefe books, as to the main part of them, were not written by Mofes ; but I do contend, that a book may contain a true hiftory, though we know not the author of it, or though we may be miftaken in afcribing it to a wrong author.

The firft argument you produce againft Mofes being the author of thefe books is fo old that I do not know its original author; and it is fo miferable an one, that I wonder you fhould adopt it——" Thefe books cannot be written by Mofes, becaufe they are written in the third perfon—it is always, The Lord faid unto Mofes, or Mofes faid unto the Lord. This, you fay, is the ftyle and manner that hiftorians ufe in fpeaking of the perfons whofe lives and actions they are writing." This obfervation is true, but it does not extend far enough; for this is the ftyle and manner not only of hiftorians writing of other perfons, but of eminent men, fuch as *Xenophon* and *Jofephus*, writing of themfelves. If General *Wafhington* fhould write the hiftory of the American war, and fhould, from his great modefty, fpeak of himfelf in the third perfon, would you think it reafonable that, two or three thoufand years hence, any perfon fhould, on that account, contend, that the hiftory was not true? *Cæfar* writes of himfelf in the third perfon—it is always, Cæfar made a fpeech, or a fpeech was made to Cæfar; Cæfar croffed the Rhine; Cæfar invaded Britain; but every fchoolboy knows that this circumftance cannot be adduced as a ferious argument againft Cæfar's being the author of his own Commentaries.

But Mofes, you urge, cannot be the author of the book of Numbers,—becaufe, he fays of himfelf——" that Mofes was a very meek man, above all the men that were on the face of the earth." If he faid this of himfelf, he was, you fay, " a vain and arrogant coxcomb, (fuch is your phrafe!) and unworthy of credit—and if he did not fay it, the *books* are without authority." This your dilemma is perfectly harmlefs; it has not an horn to hurt the weakeft logician. If Mofes did not write this little verfe, if it was inferted by Samuel, or any of his countrymen, who knew his character and revered his memory, will it follow that he did not write any other part of the book of Numbers? Or if he did not write any part of the book of Numbers, will it follow that he did not write any of the other books of which he is ufually reputed the author? And if he did write this of himfelf, he was juftified by the occafion which extorted from him this commendation. Had this expreffion been written in a modern ftyle and manner, it would probably have given you no offence. For who would be fo faftidious as to find fault with an illuftrious man, who, being calumniated by his neareft relations, as guilty of pride, and fond of power, fhould vindicate his character by faying, My temper was naturally as meek and unaffuming as that of any man upon earth? There are occafions, in which a modeft man, who fpeaks truly, may fpeak proudly of himfelf, without forfeiting his general character; and there is no occafion, which either more requires, or more excufes this conduct, than when he is repelling the foul and envious afperfions of thofe who both knew his cha-racter and had experienced his kindnefs; and in that predicament ftood *Aaron* and *Miriam,* the accufers of Mofes. You yourfelf have, probably, felt the ftings of calumny, and have been anxious to remove the impreffion. I do not call you a vain and arrogant coxcomb for vindi-cating your character, when in the latter part of this very work you boaft, and I hope truly, " that the man does not exift that can fay, I have perfecuted him, or any man, or any fet of men, in the American revolution, or in the French revolution; or that I have in any cafe returned evil for evil." I know not what kings and priefts may fay to this; you may not have returned to them evil for evil, becaufe they never, I believe, did you any harm; but you have done them all the harm you could, and that without provocation.

I think it needlefs to notice your obfervation upon what you call the dramatic ftyle of Deuteronomy; it is an ill-founded hypothefis. You might as well afk where the author of Cæfar's Commentaries got the fpeeches of Cæfar, as where the author of Deuteronomy got the fpeeches of Mofes. But your argument—that Mofes was not the author of Deuteronomy, becaufe the reafon given in that book for the obfervation of the fabbath, is different from that given in Exodus, merits a reply.

You need not be told that the very name of this book imports, in Greek, a repetition of a law; and that the Hebrew doctors have called it by a word of the fame meaning. In the fifth verfe of the firft chapter it is faid in our Bibles, " Mofes began to declare this law ;" but the Hebrew words more properly tranflated, import that Mofes " began, or determined, to explain the law." This is no fhift of mine to get over a difficulty ; the words are fo rendered in moft of the ancient verfions, and by *Fagius, Vatablus,* and *Le Clerc,* men eminently fkilled in the Hebrew language. This repetition and explanation of the law, was a wife and benevolent proceeding in Mofes; that thofe who were either not born, or were mere infants, when it was firft (forty years before) delivered in Horeb, might have an opportunity of knowing it; efpecially as Mofes their leader was foon to be taken from them, and they were about to be fettled in the midft of nations given to idolatry, and funk in vice. Now where is the wonder, that fome variations, and fome additions, fhould be made to a law, when a legiflator thinks fit to republifh it many years after its firft promulgation ?

With refpect to the fabbath, the learned are divided in opinion concerning its origin ; fome contending that it was fanctified from the creation of the world ; that it was obferved by the patriarchs before the Flood ; that it was neglected by the Ifraelites during their bondage in Egypt, revived on the falling of manna in the wildernefs, and enjoined, as a pofitive law, at Mount Sinai. Others efteem its inftitution to have been no older than the age of Mofes ; and argue, that what is faid of the fanctification of the fabbath in the book of Genefis, is faid by way of anticipation. There may be truth in both thefe accounts. To me it is probable, that the memory of the Creation was handed down from Adam to all his pofterity ; and that the feventh day was, for a long time, held facred by all nations, in commemoration of that event; but that the

peculiar rigidnefs of its obfervance was enjoined by Mofes
to the Ifraelites alone. As to there being two reafons
given for its being kept holy,——one, that on that day God
refted from the work of creation——the other, that on that
day God had given them reft from the fervitude of
Egypt——I fee no contradiction in the accounts. If a
man, in writing the hiftory of England, fhould inform his
readers, that the parliament had ordered the fifth of
November to be kept holy, becaufe on that day God had
delivered the nation from a bloody intended maffacre by
gunpowder; and if, in another part of his hiftory, he
fhould affign the deliverance of our church and nation
from popery and arbitrary power, by the arrival of King
William, as a reafon for its being kept holy; would any
one contend, that he was not juftified in both thefe ways
of expreffion, or that we ought from thence to conclude,
that he was not the author of them both ?

You think——" that law in Deuteronomy inhuman and
brutal, which authorizes parents, the father and the mother, to bring their own children to have them ftoned to
death for what it is pleafed to call ftubbornnefs."——You
are aware, I fuppofe, that paternal power, amongft the
Romans, the *Gauls*, the *Perfians*, and other nations, was
of the moft arbitrary kind; that it extended to the taking
away the life of the child. I do not know whether the
Ifraelites in the time of Mofes exercifed this paternal
power; it was not a cuftom adopted by all nations, but it
was by many; and in the infancy of fociety, before individual families had coalefced into communities, it was
probably very general. Now Mofes, by this law, which
you efteem brutal and inhuman, hindered fuch an extravagant power from being either introduced or exercifed
amongft the Ifraelites. This law is fo far from counte-
nancing the arbitrary power of a father over the life of his
child, that it takes from him the power of accufing the
child before a magiftrate——the father and the mother of
the child muft agree in bringing the child to judgement——
and it is not by their united will that the child was to be
condemned to death; the elders of the city were to judge

whether the accufation was true; and the accufation was to be not merely, as you infinuate, that the child was ftubborn, but that he was " ftubborn and rebellious, a glutton and a drunkard." Confidered in this light, you muft allow the law to have been an humane reftriction of a power improper to be lodged with any parent.

That you may abufe the priefts, you abandon your fubject—" Priefts, you fay, preach up Deuteronomy, for Deuteronomy preaches up tithes."—I do not know that priefts preach up Deuteronomy, more than they preach up other books of Scripture; but I do know that tithes are not preached up in Deuteronomy, more than in Leviticus, in Numbers, in Chronicles, in Malachi, in the law, the hiftory, and the prophets of the Jewifh nation.——You go on—" It is from this book, chap. xxv. ver. 4, they have taken the phrafe, and applied it to tithing, Thou fhalt not muzzle the ox when he treadeth out the corn;" and that this might not efcape obfervation, they have noted it in the table of contents at the head of the chapter, though it is only a fingle verfe of lefs than two lines. " O priefts ! priefts ! ye are willing to be compared to an ox for the fake of tithes !"—I cannot call this—reafoning—and I will not pollute my page by giving it a proper appellation. Had the table of contents, inftead of fimply faying—the ox is not to be muzzled—faid—tithes enjoined, or priefts to be maintained—there would have been a little ground for your cenfure. Whoever noted this phrafe at the head of the chapter, had better reafon for doing it than you have attributed to them. They did it becaufe St. Paul had quoted it when he was proving to the Corinthians, that they who preached the gofpel had a right to live by the gofpel; it was Paul, and not the priefts who firft applied this phrafe to tithing. St. Paul, indeed, did not avail himfelf of the right he contended for; he was not, therefore, interefted in what he faid. The reafon on which he grounds the right, is not merely this quotation, which you ridicule ; nor the appointment of the law of Mofes, which you think fabulous; nor the injunction of Jefus, which you defpife ; no, it is a reafon founded in the nature of things, and which no philofopher, no unbeliever, no man of common fenfe can deny to be a folid reafon; it amounts to this — that " the labourer is worthy of his hire." Nothing is fo much a man's own, as his labour and ingenuity: and it is entirely confonant to the law of nature, that by the innocent ufe of thefe he fhould provide for his fubfiftence. Hufbandmen, artifts, foldiers, phyficians, lawyers, all let out their labour and talents for a ftipulated reward: why may not a prieft do the fame? Some accounts of you have been publifhed in England; but conceiving them to have proceeded from a defign to injure your character, I never read them. I know nothing of your parentage, your education, or condition in life. You may have been elevated, by your birth, above the neceffity of acquiring the means of fuftaining life by the labour either of hand or head; if this be the cafe, you ought not to defpife thofe who have come into the world in lefs favourable circumftances. If your origin has been lefs fortunate, you muft have fupported yourfelf, either by manual labour, or the exercife of your genius. Why fhould you think that conduct difreputable in priefts, which you probably confider as laudable in yourfelf? I know not whether you have as great a diflike of kings as of priefts; but that you may be induced to think more favourably of men of my profeffion, I will juft mention to you that the payment of tithes is no new inftitution, but that they were paid in the moft ancient times, not to priefts only, but to kings. I could give you an hundred inftances of this; two may be fufficient: *Abraham* paid tithes to the king of Salem, four hundred years before the law of Mofes was given. The king of Salem was prieft alfo of the moft high God. Priefts, you fee, exifted in the world, and were held in high eftimation, for kings were priefts, long before the impoftures, as you efteem them, of the Jewifh and Chriftian difpenfations were heard of. But as this inftance is taken from a book which you call " a book of contradictions and lies"——the Bible;——I will give you another, from a book, to the authority of which, as it is written by a profane author, you probably will not object. *Diogenes Laertius*, in his life of *Solon*, cites a letter of *Pisistratus* to that law-giver, in which he says——"I Pisistratus, the tyrant, am contented with the stipends which were paid to those who reigned before me; the people of Athens set apart a *tenth* of the fruits of their land, not for my private use, but to be expended in the public sacrifices, and for the general good."

LETTER III.

Having done with what you call the grammatical evidence that Moses was not the author of the books attributed to him, you come to your historical and chronological evidence; and you begin with Genesis. Your first argument is taken from the single word——Dan——being found in Genesis, when it appears from the book of Judges, that the town of Laish was not called Dan, till above three hundred and thirty years after the death of Moses: therefore the writer of Genesis, you conclude, must have lived after the town of Laish had the name of Dan given to it. Lest this objection should not be obvious enough to a common capacity, you illustrate it in the following manner: " Havre-de-Grace was called Havre-Marat in 1793; should then any dateless writing be found, in after-times, with the name of Havre-Marat, it would be certain evidence that such a writing could not have been written till after the year 1793." This is a wrong conclusion. Suppose some hot republican should at this day publish a new edition of any old history of France, and instead of Havre-de-Grace should write Havre-Marat; and that, two or three thousand years hence, a man, like yourself, should, on that account, reject the whole history as spurious, would he be justified in so doing? Would it not be reasonable to tell him——that the name Havre-Marat had been inserted, not by the original author of the history, but

by a fubfequent editor of it ; and to refer him, for a proof
of the genuinenefs of the book, to the teftimony of the
whole French nation ? This fuppofition fo obvioufly applies to your difficulty, that I cannot but recommend it to
your impartial attention. But if this folution does not
pleafe you, I defire it may be proved, that the *Dan*, mentioned in Genefis, was the fame town as the *Dan*, mentioned in Judges. I defire, further, to have it proved, that
the Dan mentioned in Genefis, was the name of a town,
and not of a river. It is merely faid—Abraham purfued
them, the enemies of Lot, to Dan. Now a river was full
as likely as a town to ftop a purfuit. *Lot*, we know, was
fettled in the plain of *Jordan;* and Jordan, we know, was
compofed of the united ftreams of two rivers, called *Jor*
and *Dan.*

Your next difficulty refpects its being faid in Genefis—
" Thefe are the kings that reigned in *Edom* before there
reigned any king over the children of Ifrael ;—this paffage
could only have been written, you fay (and I think you
fay rightly), after the firft king began to reign over Ifrael ;
fo far from being written by Mofes, it could not have been
written till the time of Saul at the leaft." I admit this inference, but I deny its application. A fmall addition to a
book does not deftroy either the genuinenefs or the authenticity of the whole book. I am not ignorant of the
manner in which commentators have anfwered this objection of Spinoza, without making the conceffion which I
have made ; but I have no fcruple in admitting, that the
paffage in queftion, confifting of nine verfes containing the
genealogy of fome kings of Edom, might have been inferted in the book of Genefis, after the book of Chronicles
(which was called in Greek by a name importing that it
contained things left out in other books) was written.
The learned have fhewn, that interpolations have happened
to other books ; but thefe infertions by other hands have
never been confidered as invalidating the authority of thofe
books.

" Take away from Genefis," you fay, " the belief that
Mofes was the author, on which only the ftrange belief

that it is the word of God has ftood, and there remains nothing of Genefis but an anonymous book of ftories, fables, traditionary or invented abfurdities, or of downright lies."——What! is it a ftory then, that the world had a beginning, and that the author of it was God? If you deem this a ftory, I am not difputing with a deiftical philofopher, but with an atheiftic madman. Is it a ftory, that our firft parents fell from a paradifaical ftate——that this earth was deftroyed by a deluge—that Noah and his family were preferved in the ark——and that the world has been repeopled by his defcendants?—Look into a book fo common that almoft every body has it, and fo excellent that no perfon ought to be without it——Grotius on the Truth of the Chriftian Religion——and you will there meet with abundant teftimony to the truth of all the principal facts recorded in Genefis. The teftimony is not that of *Jews,* Chriftians, and priefts; it is the teftimony of the philofophers, hiftorians, and poets of antiquity. The oldeft book in the world is Genefis; and it is remarkable that thofe books which come neareft to it in age, are thofe which make, either the moft diftinct mention of, or the moft evident allufion to, the facts related in Genefis concerning the formation of the world from a chaotic mafs, the primeval innocence and fubfequent fall of man, the longevity of mankind in the firft ages of the world, the depravity of the antediluvians, and the deftruction of the world.—Read the tenth chapter of Genefis.——It may appear to you to contain nothing but an uninterefting narration of the defcendants of *Shem, Ham,* and *Japheth;* a mere fable, an invented abfurdity, a downright lie. No, Sir, it is one of the moft valuable, and the moft venerable records of antiquity. It explains what all profane hiftorians were ignorant of——the origin of nations. Had it told us, as other books do, that one nation had fprung out of the earth they inhabited; another from a cricket or a grafshopper; another from an oak; another from a mufhroom; another from a dragon's tooth; then indeed it would have merited the appellation you, with fo much temerity, beftow upon it. Inftead of thefe abfurdities, it

C

gives fuch an account of the peopling the earth after the
deluge, as no other book in the world ever did give; and
the truth of which all other books in the world, which
contain any thing on the fubject, confirm. The laft verfe
of the chapter fays——" Thefe are the families of the fons
of Noah, after their generations, in their nations: and by
thefe were the nations divided in the earth, after the
flood." It would require great learning to trace out, pre-
cifely, either the actual fituation of all the countries in
which thefe founders of empires fettled, or to afcertain
the extent of their dominions. This, however, has been
done by various authors, to the fatisfaction of all competent judges; fo much at leaft to my fatisfaction, that
had I no other proof of the authenticity of Genefis, I
fhould confider this as fufficient. But, without the aid
of learning, any man who can barely read his Bible, and
has but heard of fuch people as the *Affyrians*, the *Elamites*,
the *Lydians*, the *Medes*, the *Ionians*, the *Thracians*, will
readily acknowledge that they had *Affur*, and *Elam*, and
Lud, and *Madai*, and *Javan*, and *Tiros*, grandfons of *Noah*,
for their refpective founders; and knowing this, he will
not, I hope, part with his Bible, as a fyftem of fables.
I am no enemy to philofophy; but when philofophy
would rob me of my Bible, I muft fay of it, as Cicero
faid of the twelve tables,——This little book alone exceeds
the libraries of all the philofophers in the weight of its
authority, and in the extent of its utility.

   From the abufe of the Bible, you proceed to that of
Mofes, and again bring forward the fubject of his wars in
the land of Canaan. There are many men who look upon
all war (would to God that all men faw it in the fame
light!) with extreme abhorrence, as afflicting mankind
with calamities not neceffary, fhocking to humanity, and
repugnant to reafon. But is it repugnant to reafon that
God fhould, by an exprefs act of his providence, deftroy a
wicked nation? I am fond of confidering the goodnefs of
God as the leading principle of his conduct towards mankind, of confidering his juftice as fubfervient to his mercy.
He punifhes individuals and nations with the rod of his

wrath; but I am perfuaded that all his punifhments origi-
nate in his abhorrence of fin; are calculated to leffen its
influence; and are proofs of his goodnefs; inafmuch as it
may not be poffible for Omnipotence itfelf to communi-
cate fupreme happinefs to the human race, whilft they
continue fervants of fin. The deftruction of the Canaanites exhibits to all nations, in all ages, a fignal proof of
God's difpleafure againft fin; it has been to others, and it
is to ourfelves, a benevolent warning. Mofes would have
been the wretch you reprefent him, had he acted by his
own authority alone; but you may as reafonably attribute
cruelty and murder to the judge of the land in condem-
ning criminals to death, as butchery and maffacre to
Mofes in executing the command of God.

The Midianites, through the counfel of Balaam, and
by the vicious inftrumentality of their women, had
feduced a part of the Ifraelites to idolatry; to the impure
worfhip of their infamous god Baalpeor:—for this offence,
twenty-four thoufand Ifraelites had perifhed in a plague
from heaven, and Mofes received a command from God
"to fmite the Midianites who had beguiled the people."
An army was equipped, and fent againft Midian. When
the army returned victorious, Mofes and the princes of
the congregation went to meet it; " and Mofes was wroth
with the officers." He obferved the women captives, and
he afked with aftonifhment: " Have ye faved all the
women alive? Behold, thefe caufed the children of Ifrael,
through the counfel of Balaam, to commit trefpafs againft
the Lord in the matter of Peor, and there was a plague
among the congregation." He then gave an order that
the boys and the women fhould be put to death, but
that the young maidens fhould be kept alive for themfelves. I fee nothing in this proceeding, but good policy,
combined with mercy. The young men might have
become dangerous avengers of, what they would efteem,
their country's wrongs; the mothers might have again
allured the Ifraelites to the love of licentious pleafures
and the practice of idolatry, and brought another plague
upon the congregation; but the young maidens, not being

polluted by the flagitious habits of their mothers, nor
likely to create disturbance by rebellion, were kept alive.
You give a different turn to the matter; you say—"that
thirty-two thousand women-children were configned to
debauchery by the order of Mofes."——Prove this, and I
will allow that Mofes was the horrid monfter you make
him——prove this, and I will allow that the Bible is what
you call it—"a book of lies, wickedness, and blafphemy."
——Prove this, or excufe my warmth if I fay to you, as
Paul faid to Elymas the forcerer, who fought to turn
away Sergius Paulus from the faith, " O full of all fub-
tilty, and all mifchief, thou child of the devil, thou enemy
of all righteoufnefs, wilt thou not ceafe to pervert the
right ways of the Lord ?"——I did not, when I began
thefe letters, think that I fhould have been moved to this
feverity of rebuke, by any thing you could have written ;
but when fo grofs a mifreprefentation is made of God's
proceedings, coolnefs would be a crime. The women-
children were not referved for the purpofes of debauchery, but of flavery; a cuftom abhorrent from our manners,
but every where practifed in former times, and ftill practifed in countries where the benignity of the chriftian
religion has not foftened the ferocity of human nature.
You here admit a part of the account given in the Bible
refpecting the expedition againft Midian to be a true
account; it is not unreafonable to defire that you will
admit the whole, or fhew fufficient reafon why you
admit one part, and reject the other. I will mention the
part to which you have paid no attention. The Ifraelitifh
army confifted but of twelve thoufand men, a mere
handful when oppofed to the people of Midian; yet,
when the officers made a mufter of their troops after their
return from the war, they found that they had not loft a
fingle man ! This circumftance ftruck them as fo decifive
an evidence of God's interpofition, that out of the fpoils
they had taken they offered " an oblation to the Lord,
an atonement for their fouls." Do but believe what the
captains of thoufands, and the captains of hundreds,
believed at the time when thefe things happened, and we

fhall never more hear of your objection to the Bible, from its account of the wars of Mofes.

You produce two or three other objections refpecting the genuinenefs of the firft five books of the Bible.——I cannot ftop to notice them: every commentator anfwers them in a manner fuited to the apprehenfion of even a mere Englifh reader. You calculate, to the thoufandth part of an inch, the length of the iron bed of *Og* the king of Bafan; but you do not prove that the bed was too big for the body, or that a Patagonian would have been loft in it. You make no allowance for the fize of a royal bed; nor ever fufpect that king Og might have been poffeffed with the fame kind of vanity, which occupied the mind of king Alexander, when he ordered his foldiers to enlarge the fize of their beds, that they might give to the Indians, in fucceeding ages, a great idea of the prodigious ftature of a Macedonian. In many parts of your work you fpeak much in commendation of fcience. I join with you in every commendation you can give it; but you fpeak of it in fuch a manner as gives room to believe, that you are a great proficient in it; if this be the cafe, I would recommend a problem to your attention, the folution of which you will readily allow to be far above the powers of a man converfant only, as you reprefent priefts and bifhops to be, in *hic, hæc, hoc.* The problem is this——To determine the height to which a human body, preferving its fimilarity of figure, may be augmented, before it will perifh by its own weight.—— When you have folved this problem, we fhall know whether the bed of the king of Bafan was too big for any giant; whether the exiftence of a man twelve or fifteen feet high is in the nature of things impoffible. My philofophy teaches me to doubt of many things; but it does not teach me to reject every teftimony which is oppofite to my experience: had I been born in Shetland, I could, on proper teftimony, have believed in the exiftence of the Lincolnfhire ox, or of the largeft drayhorfe in London; though the oxen and horfes in Shetland had not been bigger than maftiffs.

LETTER IV.

H<small>AVING</small> finifhed your objections to the genuinenefs of the book of Mofes, you proceed to your remarks on the book of Jofhua; and from its internal evidence you endeavour to prove, that this book was not written by Jofhua.——What then? what is your conclufion?—"That it is anonymous and without authority."——Stop a little; your conclufion is not connected with your premifes; your friend Euclid would have been afhamed of it: "Anonymous, and therefore without authority!" I have noticed this folecifm before; but as you frequently bring it forward, and, indeed, your book ftands much in need of it, I will fubmit to your confideration another obfervation upon the fubject. The book called Fleta is anonymous, but it is not on that account without authority.——Doomf-day book is anonymous, and was written above feven hundred years ago; yet our courts of law do not hold it to be without authority, as to the matters of fact related in it. Yes, you will fay, but this book has been preferved with fingular care amongft the records of the nation. And who told you that the Jews had no records, or that they did not preferve them with fingular care? Jofephus fays the contrary; and, in the Bible itfelf, an appeal is made to many books, which have perifhed; fuch as the book of Jafher, the book of Nathan, of Abijah, of Iddo, of Jehu, of the natural hiftory of Solomon, of the acts of Manaffeh, and others which might be mentioned. If any one having accefs to the journals of the lords and commons, to the books of the treafury, war-office, privy-council, and other public documents, fhould at this day write an hiftory of the reigns of George the Firft and Second, and fhould publifh it without his name, would any man, three or four hundreds or thoufands of years hence, queftion the authority of that book, when he knew that the whole Britifh nation had received it as an authentic book, from the time of its firft publication to the age in which he

lived ? This fuppofition is in point. The books of the
Old Teftament were compofed from the records of the
Jewifh nation, and they have been received as true by that
nation, from the time in which they were written to the
prefent day. Dodfley's Annual Regifter is an anonymous
book, we only know the name of its editor;. the New
Annual Regifter is an anonymous book; the Reviews are
anonymous books; but do we, or will our pofterity, efteem thefe books as of no authority? On the contrary,
they are admitted at prefent, and will be received in after-
ages, as authoritative records of the civil, military, and
literary hiftory of England and of Europe. So little foundation is there for our being ftartled by your affertion,
" It is anonymous and without authority."

If I am right in this reafoning, (and I proteft to you
that I do not fee any error in it,) all the arguments you
adduce in proof that the book of Jofhua was not written
by Jofhua, nor that of Samuel by Samuel, are nothing to
the purpofe for which you have brought them forward:
thefe books may be books of authority, though all you
advance againft the genuinenefs of them fhould be granted.
No article of faith is injured by allowing that there is no
fuch pofitive proof, when or by whom thefe, and fome other
books of Holy Scripture, were written, as to exclude all
poffibility of doubt and cavil. There is no neceffity, indeed, to allow this. The chronological and hiftorical difficulties, which others before you have produced, have been
anfwered, and as to the greateft part of them, fo well anfwered, that I will not wafte the reader's time by entering
into a particular examination of them.

You make yourfelf merry with what you call the tale
of the fun ftanding ftill upon mount Gibeon, and the
moon in the valley of Ajalon; and you fay that "the
ftory detects itfelf, becaufe there is not a nation in the
world that knows any thing about it." How can you
expect that there fhould, when there is not a nation in the
world whofe annals reach this æra by many hundred
years? It happens, however, that you are probably miftaken as to the fact: a confufed tradition concerning this

miracle, and a fimilar one in the time of Hezekiah, when
the fun went back ten degrees, had been preferved among
one of the moft ancient nations, as we are informed by
one of the moft ancient hiftorians. Herodotus, in his
Euterpe, fpeaking of the Egyptian priefts, fays——" They
told me that the fun four times deviated from his courfe,
having twice rifen where he uniformly goes down, and
twice gone down where he uniformly rifes. This however had produced no alteration in the climate of Egypt,
the fruits of the earth and the phænomena of the Nile had
always been the fame." (Beloe's Tranfl.) The laft part
of this obfervation confirms the conjecture, that this account of the Egyptian priefts had a reference to the two
miracles refpecting the fun mentioned in Scripture; for
they were not of that kind, which could introduce any
change in climates or feafons. You would have been contented to admit the account of this miracle as a fine piece
of poetical imagery;——you may have feen fome Jewifh
doctors and fome Chriftian commentators, who confider it
as fuch; but improperly in my opinion. I think it idle, at
leaft, if not impious, to undertake to explain how the miracle was performed; but one who is not able to explain
the mode of doing a thing, argues ill if he thence infers
that the thing was not done. We are perfectly ignorant
how the fun was formed, how the planets were projected
at the creation, how they are ftill retained in their orbits
by the power of gravity; but we admit, notwithftanding,
that the fun was formed, that the planets were then projected, and that they are ftill retained in their orbits. The
machine of the univerfe is in the hand of God; he can
ftop the motion of any part, or of the whole of it, with
lefs trouble and lefs danger of injuring it, than you can
ftop your watch. In teftimony of the reality of the miracle, the author of the book fays—" Is this not written in
the book of Jafher?——No author in his fenfes would
have appealed in proof of his veracity, to a book which
did not exift, or in atteftation of a fact, which, though it
did exift, was not recorded in it; we may fafely therefore
conclude that, at the time the book of Jofhua was written.

there was such a book as the book of Jasher, and that the miracle of the sun's standing still was recorded in that book. But this observation, you will say, does not prove the fact of the sun's having stood still; I have not produced it as a proof of that fact; but it proves that the author of the book of Joshua believed the fact, and that the people of Israel admitted the authority of the book of Jasher. An appeal to a fabulous book would have been as senseless an insult upon their understanding, as it would have been upon ours, had Rapin appealed to the Arabian Nights' Entertainment, as a proof of the battle of Hastings.

I cannot attribute much weight to your argument against the genuineness of the book of Joshua, from its being said that——" Joshua burned Ai, and made it an heap for ever, even a desolation unto *this day*." Joshua lived twenty-four years after the burning of Ai: and if he wrote his history in the latter part of his life, what absurdity is there in saying, Ai is still in ruins, or Ai is in ruins to this very day. A young man who had seen the heads of the rebels, in forty-five, when they were first stuck upon poles at Temple Bar, might, twenty years afterwards, in attestation of his veracity in speaking of the fact, have justly said——And they are there to this very day. Whoever wrote the gospel of St. Matthew, it was written not many centuries, probably (I had almost said certainly) not a quarter of one century after the death of Jesus; yet the author, speaking of the Potter's field which had been purchased by the chief priests with the money they had given Judas to betray his master, says, that it was therefore called the field of blood *unto this day;* and in another place he says, that the story of the body of Jesus being stolen out of the sepulchre was commonly reported among the Jews *until this day.* Moses, in his old age, had made use of a similar expression, when he put the Israelites in mind of what the Lord had done to the Egyptians in the Red Sea, " The Lord hath destroyed them unto this day." (Deut. xi. 4.)

In the last chapter of the book of Joshua it is related, that Joshua assembled all the tribes of Israel to Shechem;

and there, in the prefence of the elders and principal men of Ifrael, he recapitulated, in a fhort fpeech, all that God had done for their nation, from the calling of Abraham to that time, when they were fettled in the land which God had promifed to their forefathers. In finifhing his fpeech, he faid to them——"Choofe you this day whom you will ferve, whether the gods which your fathers ferved, that were on the other fide of the flood, or the gods of the Amorites, in whofe land ye dwell; but as for me and my houfe, we will ferve the Lord. And the people anfwered and faid, God forbid that we fhould forfake the Lord to ferve other gods." Jofhua urged farther, that God would not fuffer them to worfhip other gods in fellowfhip with him; they anfwered that "they would ferve the Lord." Jofhua then faid to them, "Ye are witneffes againft your-felves that ye have chofen you the Lord to ferve him. And they faid, We are witneffes." Here was a folemn covenant between Jofhua, on the part of the Lord, and all the men of Ifrael, on their own part.——The text then fays ——"So Jofhua made a covenant with the people that day, and fet them a ftatute and an ordinance in Shechem, *and Jofhua wrote thefe words in the book of the Law of God.*" Here is a proof of two things——firft, that there was then, a few years after the death of Mofes, exifting a book called The book of the Law of God; the fame, without doubt, which Mofes had written, and committed to the cuftody of the Levites, that it might be kept in the ark of the covenant of the Lord, that it might be a witness againft them——fecondly, that Jofhua *wrote* a part at leaft of his own tranfactions in that very book, as an addition to it. It is not a proof that he wrote all his own tranfactions in any book; but I fubmit entirely to the judgment of every candid man, whether this proof of his having recorded a very material tranfaction, does not make it probable that he recorded other material tranfactions; that he wrote the chief part of the book of Jofhua; and that·fuch things as happened after his death, have been inferted in it·by others, in order to render the hiftory more complete.

The book of Jofhua, chap. vi. ver. 26, is quoted in the

firſt book of Kings, chap. xvi. ver. 44. "In his (Ahab's) days did Hiel the Bethelite build Jericho: he laid the foundation thereof in Abiram his firſt-born, and ſet up the gates thereof in his youngeſt ſon Segub, according to the word of the Lord, which he ſpake by Joſhua the ſon of Nun." Here is a proof that the book of Joſhua is older than the firſt book of Kings; but that is not all which may be reaſonably inferred, I do not ſay proved, from this quotation.——It may be inferred from the phraſe—according to the word of the Lord, which he ſpake by Joſhua the ſon of Nun—that Joſhua *wrote down* the word which the Lord had ſpoken. In Baruch (which, though an apocryphal book, is authority for this purpoſe) there is a ſimilar phraſe—as thou ſpakeſt by thy ſervant Moſes in the day when thou didſt command him *to write thy law.*

I think it unneceſſary to make any obſervations on what you ſay relative to the book of Judges; but I cannot paſs unnoticed your cenſure of the book of Ruth, which you call "an idle bungling ſtory, fooliſhly told, nobody knows by whom, about a ſtrolling country girl creeping ſlily to bed to her couſin Boaz; pretty ſtuff, indeed," you exclaim, "to be called the word of God!"—It ſeems to me that you do not perfectly comprehend what is meant by the expreſſion—the word of God—or the divine authority of the Scriptures:——I will explain it to you in the words of Dr. Law, late biſhop of Carliſle, and in thoſe of St. Auſtin. My firſt quotation is from biſhop Law's Theory of Religion, a book not undeſerving your notice.— " The true ſenſe then of the *divine authority* of the books of the Old Teſtament, and which, perhaps, is enough to denominate them in general *divinely inſpired,* ſeems to be this; that as in thoſe times God has all along, beſide the inſpection, or ſuperintendency of his general providence, interfered upon particular occaſions, by giving expreſs commiſſions to ſome perſons (thence called *prophets*) to declare his will in various manners, and degrees of evidence, as beſt ſuited the occaſion, time, and nature of the ſubject; and in all other caſes, left them wholly to themſelves: in like manner, he has interpoſed his more immediate aſſiſt-

ance, and notified it to them, as they did to the world,) in
the *recording* of thefe revelations; fo far as that was neceffary, amidft the common (but from hence termed *facred*)
hiftory of thofe times; and mixed with various other occur-
rences; in which the hiftorian's own natural qualifications
were fufficient to enable him to relate things, with all the
accuracy they required."——The paffage from St. Auftin is
this——" I am of opinion, that thofe men, to whom the
Holy Ghoft revealed what ought to be received as authoritative in religion, might write fome things as men with
hiftorical diligence, and other things as prophets by divine
infpiration; and that thefe things are fo diftinct, that the
former may be attributed to themfelves as contributing
to the increafe of knowledge, and the latter to God
fpeaking by them things appertaining to the authority
of religion." Whether this opinion be right or wrong,
I do not here inquire; it is the opinion of many learned
men and good Chriftians; and if you will adopt it as
your opinion, you will fee caufe, perhaps, to become
a Chriftian yourfelf; you will fee caufe to confider
chronological, geographical, or genealogical errors——
apparent miftakes or real contradictions as to hiftorical
facts——needlefs repetitions and trifling interpolations——
indeed you will fee caufe to confider all the principal objections of your book to be abfolutely without foundation.
Receive but the Bible as compofed by upright and well
informed, though in fome points, fallible men, (for I exclude all fallibility when they profefs to deliver the word
of God,) and you muft receive it as a book revealing to
you, in many parts, the exprefs will of God; and in other
parts, relating to you the ordinary hiftory of the times.
Give but the authors of the Bible that credit which you
give to other hiftorians; believe them to deliver the word
of God, when they tell you that they do fo; believe when
they relate other things as of themfelves, and not of the
Lord, that they wrote to the beft of their knowledge and
capacity; and you will be in your belief fomething very
different from a deift: you may not be allowed to afpire
to the character of an orthodox believer, but you will not

be an unbeliever in the divine authority of the Bible; though you fhould admit human miftakes and human opinions to exift in fome parts of it. This I take to be the firft ftep towards the removal of the doubts of many fceptical men; and when they are advanced thus far, the grace of God, affifting a teachable difpofition, and a pious intention, may carry them on to perfection.

As to Ruth, you do an injury to her character. She was not a ftrolling country girl. She had been married ten years; and being left a widow without children, fhe accompanied her mother-in-law, returning into her native country, out of which with her hufband and her two fons fhe had been driven by a famine. The difturbances in France have driven many men with their families to America; if, ten years hence, a woman, having loft her hufband and her children, fhould return to France with a daughter-in-law, would you be juftified in calling the daughter-in-law a ftrolling country girl?——But fhe "crept flily to bed to her coufin Boaz."——I do not find it fo in the hiftory——as a perfon imploring protection, fhe laid herfelf down at the foot of an aged kinfman's bed, and fhe rofe up with as much innocence as fhe had laid herfelf down; fhe was afterwards married to Boaz, and reputed by all her neighbours a virtuous woman; and they were more likely to know her character than you are. Whoever reads the book of Ruth, bearing in mind the fimplicity of ancient manners, will find it an interefting ftory of a poor young woman following, in a ftrange land, the advice, and affectionately attaching herfelf to the fortunes, of the mother of her deceafed hufband.

The two books of Samuel come next under your review. You proceed to fhew that thefe books were not written by Samuel, that they are anonymous, and thence you conclude without authority. I need not here repeat what I have faid upon the fallacy of your conclufion; and as to your proving that the books were not written by Samuel, you might have fpared yourfelf fome trouble, if you had recollected, that it is generally admitted, that Samuel did not write any part of the fecond book which

D

bears his name, and only a part of the firſt. It would, indeed, have been an inquiry not undeſerving your notice, in many parts of your work, to have examined what was the opinion of learned men reſpecting the authors of the ſeveral books of the Bible; you would have found, that you were in many places fighting a phantom of your own raiſing, and proving what was generally admitted. Very little certainty, I think, can at this time be obtained on this ſubject; but that you may have ſome knowledge of what has been conjectured by men of judgment, I will quote to you a paſſage from Dr. Hartley's Obſervations on Man. The author himſelf does not vouch for the truth of his obſervation, for he begins it with a ſuppoſition. ——" I ſuppoſe then, that the Pentateuch conſiſts of the writings of *Moſes*, put together by *Samuel*, with a very few additions; that the books of Joſhua and Judges were, in like manner, collected by him; and the book of Ruth, with the firſt part of the firſt book of Samuel, written by him; that the latter part of the firſt book of Samuel, and the ſecond book, were written by the prophets who ſucceeded Samuel, ſuppoſe *Nathan* and *Gad ;* that the book of Kings and Chronicles are extracts from the records of the ſucceeding prophets, concerning their own times, and from the public genealogical tables, made by *Ezra ;* that the books of Ezra and Nehemiah are collections of like re-cords, ſome written by *Ezra* and *Nehemiah*, and ſome by their predeceſſors ; that the book of Eſther was written by ſome eminent Jew, in or near the times of the tranſ-action there recorded, perhaps *Mordecai ;* the book of Job by a Jew, of an uncertain time; the Pſalms by *David,* and other pious perſons; the books of Proverbs and Canticles by *Solomon ;* the book of Eccleſiaſtes by *Solomon*, or perhaps by a Jew of later times, ſpeaking in his perſon, but not with an intention to make him paſs for the author; the prophecies by the prophets whoſe names they bear ; and the books of the New Teſtament by the perſons to whom they are uſually aſcribed."——I have produced this paſſage to you, not merely to ſhew you that, in a great part of your work, you are attacking what no perſon is intereſted in defending ; but to convince you that a wife and good man, and a firm believer in revealed religion, for fuch was Dr. Hartley, and no prieft, did not reject the anonymous books of the Old Teftament as books without authority. I fhall not trouble either you or myfelf with any more obfervations on that head; you may afcribe the two books of Kings, and the two books of Chronicles, to what authors you pleafe; I am fatisfied with knowing that the annals of the Jewifh nation were written in the time of Samuel, and, probably, in all fucceeding times, by men of ability, who lived in or near the times in which they write. Of the truth of this obfervation we have abundant proof, not only from the teftimony of Jofephus, and of the writers of the Talmuds, but from the Old Teftament itfelf. I will content myfelf with citing a few places——" Now the acts of David the king, firft and laft, behold they are written in the book of Samuel the feer, and in the book of Nathan the prophet, and in the book of Gad the feer." 1 Chron. xxix. 29. ——" Now the reft of the acts of Solomon, firft and laft, are they not written in the book of Nathan the prophet, and in the prophecy of Ahijah the Shilonite, and in the vifions of Iddo the feer?" 2 Chron. ix. 29.——" Now the acts of Rehoboam, firft and laft, are they not written in the book of Shemaiah the prophet, and of Iddo the feer, concerning genealogies?" 2 Chron. xii. 15.——" Now the reft of the acts of Jehofhaphat, firft and laft, behold they are written in the book of Jehu the fon of Hanani." 2 Chron. xx. 34. Is it poffible for writers to give a ftronger evidence of their veracity than by referring their readers to the books from which they had extracted the materials of their hiftory?

"The two books of Kings," you fay, "are little more than an hiftory of affaffinations, treachery, and war." That the kings of Ifrael and Judah were many of them very wicked perfons, is evident from the hiftory which is given of them in the Bible; but it ought to be remembered that their wickednefs is not to be attributed to their religion; nor were the people of Ifrael chofen to be the people of God, on account of their wickednefs; nor was their being chofen, a caufe of it. One may wonder, indeed, that, having experienced fo many fingular marks of God's goodnefs towards their nation, they did not at once become, and continue to be, (what, however, they have long been,) ftrenuous advocates for the worfhip of one only God, the Maker of heaven and earth. This was the purpofe for which they were chofen, and this purpofe has been accomplifhed. For above three and twenty hundred years the Jews have uniformly witneffed to all the nations of the earth the unity of God, and his abomination of idolatry. But as you look upon " the appellation of the Jews being God's *chofen* people as a *lie*, which the priefts and leaders of the Jews had invented to cover the bafenefs of their own characters, and which Chriftian priefts, fometimes as corrupt, and often as cruel, have profeffed to believe," I will plainly ftate to you the reafons which induce me to believe that it is no *lie*, and I hope they will be fuch reafons as you will not attribute either to cruelty or corruption.

To any one contemplating the univerfality of things, and the fabric of nature, this globe of earth, with the men dwelling on its furface, will not appear (exclufive of the divinity of their fouls) of more importance than an hillock of ants; all of which, fome with corn, fome with eggs, fome without any thing, run hither and thither, buftling about a little heap of duft. — This is a thought of the immortal Bacon ; and it is admirably fitted to humble the pride of philofophy, attempting to prefcribe forms to the proceedings, and bounds to the attributes of God. We may as eafily circumfcribe infinity, as penetrate the fecret purpofes of the Almighty. There are but two ways by which I can acquire any knowledge of the nature of the Supreme Being,—by reafon, and by revelation; to you, who reject revelation, there is but one. Now my reafon informs me, that God has made a great difference between the kinds of animals, with refpect to their capacity of enjoying happinefs. Every kind is perfect in its order; but if we compare different kinds together, one will appear to be greatly fuperior to another. An animal, which has but one fenfe, has but one fource of happinefs ; but if it be fupplied with what is fuited to that fenfe, it enjoys all the happinefs of which it is capable, and is in its nature perfect. Other forts of animals, which have two or three fenfes, and which have alfo abundant means of gratifying them, enjoy twice or thrice as much happinefs as thofe do which have but one. In the fame fort of animals there is a great difference amongft individuals, one having the fenfes more perfect, and the body lefs fubject to difeafe, than another. Hence, if I were to form a judgment of the divine goodnefs by this ufe of my reafon, I could not but fay that it was partial and unequal.——"What fhall we fay then? Is God unjuft? God forbid!" His goodnefs may be unequal, without being imperfect; it muft be eftimated from the whole, and not from a part. Every order of beings is fo fufficient for its own happinefs, and fo conducive at the fame time to the happinefs of every other, that in one view it feems to be made for itfelf alone, and in another not for itfelf but for every other. Could we comprehend the whole of the immenfe fabric which God hath formed, I am perfuaded, that we fhould fee nothing but perfection, harmony, and beauty, in every part of it; but whilft we difpute about parts, we neglect the whole, and difcern nothing but fuppofed anomalies and defects. The maker of a watch, or the builder of a fhip, is not to be blamed becaufe a fpectator cannot difcover either the beauty or the ufe of difjointed parts. And fhall we dare to accufe God of injuftice, for not having diftributed the gifts of nature in the fame degree to all kinds of animals, when it is probable that this very inequality of diftribution may be the means of producing the greateft fum total of happinefs to the whole fyftem? In exactly the fame manner may we reafon concerning the acts of God's efpecial providence. If we confider any one act, fuch as that of appointing the Jews to be his peculiar people, as unconnected with every other, it may appear to be a partial difplay of his goodnefs; it may excite doubts concerning the wifdom or the benignity of his divine nature. But if we connect the hiftory of the Jews with that of other nations, from the moft remote antiquity to the prefent

time, we fhall difcover that they were not chofen fo
much for their own benefit, or on account of their own
merit, as for the general benefit of mankind. To the
Egyptians, Chaldeans, Grecians, Romans, to all the
people of the earth, they were formerly, and they are ftill
to all civilized nations, a beacon fet upon an hill, to warn
them from idolatry, to light them to the fanctuary of a
God holy, juft, and good. Why fhould we fufpect fuch
a difpenfation of being a *lie?* when even from the little
which we can underftand of it, we fee that it is founded
in wifdom, carried on for the general good, and analogous
to all that reafon teaches us concerning the nature of God.

Several things you obferve are mentioned in the book
of the Kings, fuch as the drying up of Jeroboam's hand,
the afcent of Elijah into heaven, the deftruction of the
children who mocked Elifha, and the refurrection of a
dead man; — thefe circumftances being mentioned in the
book of Kings, and not mentioned in that of Chronicles,
is a proof to you that they are lies. I efteem it a very
erroneous mode of reafoning, which, from the filence of
one author concerning a particular circumftance, infers
the want of veracity in another who mentions it. And
this obfervation is ftill more cogent, when applied to a
book which is only a fupplement to, or an abridgment of,
other books: and under this defcription the book of
Chronicles has been confidered by all writers. But though
you will not believe the miracle of the drying up of Jeroboam's hand, what can you fay to the prophecy which
was then delivered concerning the future deftruction of
the idolatrous altar of Jeroboam? The prophecy is thus
written, 1 Kings xiii. 2.——" Behold, a child fhall be born
unto the houfe of David, Jofiah by name, and upon thee
(the altar) fhall he offer the priefts of the high places."——
Here is a clear prophecy; the name, family, and office of
a particular perfon are defcribed in the year 975 (according
to the Bible chronology) before Chrift. Above 350 years
after the delivery of the prophecy, you will find, by con-
fulting the fecond book of Kings, (chap. xxiii. 15, 16.)
this prophecy fulfilled in all its parts.

You make a calculation that Genefis was not written till 800 years after Mofes, and that it is of the fame age, and you may probably think of the fame authority, as Æfop's Fables. You give what you call the evidence of this, the air of a demonftration—" It has but two ftages : ——firft, the account of the kings of Edom, mentioned in Genefis, is taken from Chronicles, and therefore the book of Genefis was written after the book of Chronicles ;—— fecondly, the book of Chronicles was not begun to be written till after Zedekiah, in whofe time Nebuchadnezzar conquered Jerufalem, 588 years before Chrift, and more than 860 years after Mofes."——Having anfwered this objection before, I might be excufed taking any more notice of it; but as you build much, in this place, upon the ftrength of your argument, I will fhew you its weaknefs, when it is properly ftated.——A *few verfes* in the book of Genefis could not be written by Mofes :——*therefore no part* of Genefis could be written by Mofes;——a child would deny you *therefore.*——Again, a few verfes in the book of Genefis could not be written by *Mofes*, becaufe they fpeak of kings of Ifrael, there having been no kings of Ifrael in the time of Mofes; and *therefore* they could not be written by *Samuel*, or by *Solomon*, or by any other perfon who lived after there were kings in Ifrael, except by the author of the book of Chronicles ;——this is alfo an illegitimate inference from your pofition.—Again, a few verfes in the book of Genefis are, word for word, the fame as a few verfes in the book of Chronicles ;—*therefore* the author of the book of Genefis muft have taken them from Chronicles ;—another lame conclufion! Why might not the author of the book of Chronicles have taken them from Genefis, as he has taken many other genealogies, fuppofing them to have been inferted in Genefis by Samuel? But where, you may afk, could Samuel, or any other perfon have found the account of the kings of Edom ? Probably, in the public records of the nation, which were certainly as open for infpection to Samuel, and the other prophets, as they were to the author of Chronicles. I hold it needlefs to employ more time on the fubject.

LETTER V.

At length you come to two books, Ezra and Nehemiah, which you allow to be genuine books, giving an
account of the return of the Jews from the Babylonian captivity, about 536 years before Chrift : but then you fay,
" Thofe accounts are nothing to us, nor to any other perfons, unlefs it be to the Jews, as a part of the hiftory of their
nation ; and there is juft as much of the Word of God in
thofe books as there is in any of the hiftories of France, or
in Rapin's Hiftory of England." Here let us ftop a moment,
and try if from your own conceffions ìt be not poffible
to confute your argument. Ezra and Nehemiah, you
grant, are genuine books—" but they are nothing to us !
——The very firft verfe of Ezra fays——the prophecy of
Jeremiah was fulfilled :—is it nothing to us to know that
Jeremiah was a true prophet ? Do but grant that the
Supreme Being communicated to any of the fons of men
a knowledge of future events, fo that their predictions
were plainly verified, and you will find little difficulty in
admitting the truth of revealed religion. Is it nothing to
us to know that, five hundred and thirty-fix years before
Chrift, the books of Chronicles, Kings, Judges, Jofhua,
Deuteronomy, Numbers, Leviticus, Exodus, Genefis, every
book the authority of which you have attacked, are all
referred to by Ezra and Nehemiah, as authentic books,
containing the hiftory of the Ifraelitifh nation from Abraham to that very time ?—Is it nothing to us to know that
the hiftory of the Jews is true ?——It is every thing to us ;
for if that hiftory be not true, Chriftianity muft be falfe.
The Jews are the root, we are branches " graffed in
amongft them ;" to them pertain " the adoption, and the
glory, and the covenants, and the giving of the law, and
the fervice of God, and the promifes ; whofe are the fathers,
and of whom, as concerning the flefh, Chrift came, who
is over all, God bleffed for ever. Amen."

The hiftory of the Old Teftament has, without doubt,
fome difficulties in it ; but a minute philofopher, who

bufies himfelf in fearching them out, whilft he neglects
to contemplate the harmony of all its parts, the wifdom
and goodnefs of God difplayed throughout the whole,
appears to me to be like a purblind man, who, in fur-
veying a picture, objects to the fimplicity of the defign,
and the beauty of the execution, from the afperities he has
difcovered in the canvas and the colouring. The hiftory of
the Old Teftament, notwithftanding the real difficulties
which occur in it, notwithftanding the fcoffs and cavils of
unbelievers, appears to me to have fuch internal evidences
of its truth, to be fo corroborated by the moft ancient
profane hiftories, fo confirmed by the prefent circumftances
of the world, that if I were not a Chriftian, I would
become a Jew. You think this hiftory to be a collection
of lies, contradictions, blafphemies: I look upon it to be
the oldeft, the trueft, the moft comprehenfive, and the
moft important hiftory in the world. I confider it as giving
more fatisfactory proofs of the being and attributes of
God, of the origin and end of human kind, than ever
were attained by the deepeft refearches of the moft enlightened philofophers. The exercife of our reafon in the
inveftigation of truths refpecting the nature of God, and
the future expectations of human kind, is highly ufeful;
but I hope I fhall be pardoned by the metaphyficians in
faying, that the chief utility of fuch difquifitions confifts
in this——that they bring us acquainted with the weaknefs
of our intellectual faculties. I do not prefume to meafure
other men by my ftandard; you may have clearer notions
than I am able to form of the infinity of fpace; of the
eternity of duration; of neceffary exiftence; of the connection between neceffary exiftence and intelligence,
between intelligence and benevolence; you may fee nothing
in the univerfe but organized matter; or, rejecting a
material, you may fee nothing but an ideal world. With
a mind weary of conjecture, fatigued by doubt, fick of
difputation, eager for knowledge, anxious for certainty,
and unable to attain it by the beft ufe of my reafon in
matters of the utmoft importance, I have long ago turned
my thoughts to an impartial examination of the proofs

on which revealed religion is grounded, and I am convinced of its truth. This examination is a fubject within the reach of human capacity; you have come to one conclufion refpecting it, I have come to another; both of us cannot be right; may God forgive him that is in an error!

You ridicule, in a note, the ftory of an angel appearing to Jofhua. Your mirth you will perceive to be mifplaced, when you confider the defign of this appearance; it was to affure Jofhua, that the fame God who had appeared to Mofes, ordering him to pull off his fhoes, becaufe he ftood on holy ground, had now appeared to himfelf. Was this no encouragement to a man who was about to engage in war with many nations? Had it no tendency to confirm his faith? Was it no leffon to him to obey, in all things, the commands of God, and to give the glory of his conquefts to the Author of them, the God of Abraham, Ifaac, and Jacob? As to your wit about pulling off the fhoe, it originates, I think, in your ignorance; you ought to have known, that this rite was an indication of reverence for the divine prefence; and that the cuftom of entering barefoot into their temples fubfifts, in fome countries, to this day.

You allow the book of Ezra to be a genuine book; but that the author of it may not efcape without a blow, you fay, that in matters of record it is not to be depended on; and as a proof of your affertion, you tell us that the total amount of the numbers who returned from Babylon does not correfpond with the particulars; and that every child may have an argument for its infidelity, you difplay the particulars, and fhew your own fkill in arithmetic, by fumming them up. And can you fuppofe that Ezra, a man of great learning, knew fo little of fcience, fo little of the loweft branch of fcience, that he could not give his readers the fum total of fixty particular fums? You know undoubtedly that the Hebrew letters denoted alfo numbers; and that there was fuch a great fimilarity between fome of thefe letters, that it was extremely eafy for a tranfcriber of a manufcript to miftake a ⟨ⱀ⟩ for a ⟨ⱂ⟩ (or 2 for 20), a ב for a כ (or 3 for 50), a ד for ר (or 4 for 200.) Now what have we to do with numerical contradictions in the Bible, but to attribute them, wherever they occur, to this obvious source of error—the inattention of the transcriber in writing one letter for another that was like it?

I should extend these letters to a length troublesome to the reader, to you, and to myself, if I answered minutely every objection you have made, and rectified every error into which you have fallen; it may be sufficient briefly to notice some of the chief. The character represented in Job under the name of Satan is, you say, " the first and the only time this name is mentioned in the Bible." Now I find this name, as denoting an enemy, frequently occurring in the Old Testament; thus 2 Sam. xix. 22. " What have I to do with you, ye sons of Zeruiah, that you should this day be adversaries unto me?" In the original it is satans unto me. Again, 1 Kings v. 4. " The Lord my God hath given me rest on every side, so that there is neither adversary, nor evil occurrent"—in the original, neither satan nor evil. I need not mention other places; these are sufficient to shew, that the word satan, denoting an adversary, does occur in various places of the Old Testament; and it is extremely probable to me, that the root satan was introduced into the Hebrew and other eastern languages, to denote an adversary, from its having been the proper name of the great enemy of mankind. I know it is an opinion of Voltaire, that the Word satan is not older than the Babylonian captivity; this is a mistake, for it is met with in the hundred and ninth Psalm, which all allow to have been written by David, long before the captivity. Now we are upon this subject, permit me to recommend to your consideration the universality of the doctrine concerning an evil being, who in the beginning of time had opposed himself, who still continues to oppose himself, to the supreme source of all good. Amongst all nations, in all ages, this opinion prevailed, that human affairs were subject to the will of the Gods, and regulated by their interposition. Hence has been derived whatever we have read of the wandering stars of the

Chaldeans, two of them beneficent, and two malignant——hence the Egyptian *Typho* and *Ofiris*——the Perfian *Arimanius* and *Oromafdes*—the Grecian *celeftial* and *infernal Jove*—the *Brama* and the *Zupay* of the Indians, Peruvians, Mexicans——the good and evil principle, by whatever names they may be called, of all other barbarous nations—and hence the ftructure of the whole book of Job, in whatever light of hiftory or drama, it be confidered. Now does it not appear reafonable to fuppofe, that an opinion fo ancient and fo univerfal has arifen from tradition concerning the fall of our firft parents; disfigured indeed, and obfcured, as all traditions muft be, by many fabulous additions?

The Jews, you tell us, "never prayed but when they were in trouble." I do not believe this of the Jews; but that they prayed more fervently when they were in trouble than at other times, may be true of the Jews, and I apprehend is true of all nations and all individuals. But "the Jews never prayed for any thing but victory, vengeance, and riches."——Read Solomon's prayer at the dedication of the temple, and blufh for your affertion,——illiberal and uncharitable in the extreme!

"It appears," you obferve, "to have been the cuftom of the heathens to perfonify both virtue and vice, by ftatues and images, as is done now-a-days both by ftatuary and by paintings; but it does not follow from this that they worfhipped them any more than we do." Not worfhipped them! What think you of the golden image which Nebuchadnezzar fet up?——Was it not worfhipped by the princes, the rulers, the judges, the people, the nations, and the languages of the Babylonian empire? Not worfhipped them! What think you of the decree of the Roman fenate for fetching the ftatue of the mother of the gods from Peffinum? Was it only that they might admire it as a piece of workmanfhip? Not worfhipped them! "What man is there that knoweth not how that the city of the Ephefians was a worfhipper of the great goddefs Diana, and of the image which fell down from Jupiter?" Not worfhipped them!——The worfhip was univerfal,

" Every nation made gods of their own, and put them in the houses of the high places, which the Samaritans had made; the men of Babylon made Succoth-benoth, and the men of Cuth made Nergal, and the men of Hamath made Aſhima, and the Avites made Nibhaz and Tartak, and the Sepharvites burned their children in fire to A̅drammelech, and Anammelech, the gods of Sepharvaim." (2 Kings, chap. xvii.) The heathens are much indebted to you for this your curious apology for their idolatry; for a mode of worſhip the moſt cruel, ſenſeleſs, impure, abominable, that can poſſibly diſgrace the faculties of the human mind. Had this your conceit occurred in ancient times, it might have ſaved *Micah's teraphims*, the *golden calves of Jeroboam, and of Aaron*, and quite ſuperſeded the neceſſity of the ſecond commandment!!! Heathen morality has had its advocates before you; the facetious gentleman who pulled off his hat to the ſtatue of Jupiter, that he might have a friend when heathen idolatry ſhould again be in repute, ſeems to have had ſome foundation for his improper humour, ſome knowledge that certain men eſteeming themſelves great philoſophers had entered into a conſpiracy to aboliſh Chriſtianity, ſome foreſight of the conſequences which will certainly attend their ſucceſs.

It is an error, you ſay, to call the Pſalms—the Pſalms of David—This error was obſerved by St. Jerome, many hundred years before you were born; his words are— " We know that they are in an error who attribute all the Pſalms to David."—You, I ſuppoſe, will not deny, that David wrote ſome of them. Songs are of various ſorts; we have hunting ſongs, drinking ſongs, fighting ſongs, love ſongs, fooliſh, wanton, wicked ſongs;—if you will have the " Pſalms of David to be nothing but a collection from different Song-writers," you muſt allow that the writers of them were inſpired by no ordinary ſpirit; that this is a collection, incapable of being degraded by the name you give it; that it greatly excels every other collection in matter and in manner. Compare the book of Pſalms with the odes of Horace or Anacreon, with the hymns of Callimachus, the golden verſes of Pythagoras,

E

the chorufes of the Greek tragedians, (no contemptible compofitions any of thefe,) and you will quickly fee how greatly it furpaffes them all, in piety of fentiment, in fublimity of expreffion, in purity of morality, and in rational theology.

As you efteem the Pfalms of David a fong-book, it is confiftent enough in you to efteem the Proverbs of Solomon a jeft-book; there have not come down to us above eight hundred of his jefts; if we had the whole three thoufand, which he wrote, our mirth would be extreme. Let us open the book, and fee what kind of jefts it contains; take the very firft as a fpecimen——" The fear of the Lord is the beginning of knowledge; but fools defpife wifdom and inftruction."—Do you perceive any jeft in this? The fear of the Lord! What Lord does Solomon mean? He means that Lord who took the pofterity of Abraham to be his peculiar people——who redeemed that people from Egyptian bondage by a miraculous interpofition of his power——who gave the law to Mofes——who commanded the Ifraelites to exterminate the nations of Canaan.—Now this Lord you will not fear; the jeft fays, you defpife wifdom and inftruction.— Let us try again——" My fon, hear the inftruction of thy father, and forfake not the law of thy mother."——If your heart has been ever touched by parental feelings, you will fee no jeft in this.——Once more——" My fon, if finners entice thee, confent thou not." Thefe are the three firft proverbs in Solomon's "jeft book;" if you read it through, it may not make you merry; I hope it will make you wife; that it will teach you, at leaft, the beginning of wifdom—the fear of that Lord whom Solomon feared. Solomon, you tell us, was witty; jefters are fometimes witty; but though all the world, from the time of the queen of Sheba, has heard of the wifdom of Solomon, his wit was never heard of before. There is a great difference, Mr. Locke teaches us, between wit and judgment, and there is a greater between wit and wifdom. Solomon " was wifer than Ethan the Ezrahite, and Heman, and Chalcol, and Darda, the fons of Mahol."—Thefe men you may think were jefters; and fo you may call the feven wife men of Greece: but you will never convince the world that Solomon, who was wifer than them all, was nothing but a witty jefter. As to the fins and debaucheries of Solomon, we have nothing to do with them but to avoid them; and to give full credit to his experience, when he preaches to us his admirable fermon on the vanity of every thing but piety and virtue.

Ifaiah has a greater fhare of your abufe than any other writer in the Old Teftament, and the reafon of it is obvious—the prophecies of Ifaiah have received fuch a full and circumftantial completion, that, unlefs you can perfuade yourfelf to confider the whole book, (a few hiftorical fketches excepted) " as one continued bombaftical rant, full of extravagant metaphor, without application, and deftitute of meaning," you muft of neceflity allow its divine authority. You compare the burden of Babylon, the burden of Moab, the burden of Damafcus, and the other denunciations of the prophet againft cities and kingdoms, to the " ftory of the knight of the burning mountain, the ftory of Cinderella, &c." I may have read thefe ftories, but I remember nothing of the fubjects of them; I have read alfo Ifaiah's burden of Babylon, and I have compared it with the paft and prefent ftate of Babylon, and the comparifon has made fuch an impreffion on my mind, that it will never be effaced from my memory. I fhall never ceafe to believe that the Eternal alone, by whom things future are more diftinctly known than paft or prefent things are by man, that the eternal God alone could have dictated to the prophet Ifaiah the fubject of the burden of Babylon.

The latter part of the forty-fourth, and the beginning of the forty-fifth chapter of Ifaiah, are, in your opinion, fo far from being written by Ifaiah, that they could only have been written by fome perfon who lived at leaft an hundred and fifty years after Ifaiah was dead:—thefe chapters, you go on, " are a compliment to Cyrus, who permitted the Jews to return to Jerufalem from the Babylonian captivity above one hundred and fifty years after

the death of Ifaiah :"——and is it for this, fir, that you
accufe the church of audacity and the priefts of ignorance,
in impofing, as you call it, this book upon the world as
the writing of Ifaiah ? What fhall be faid of you, who,
either defignedly or ignorantly, reprefent one of the moft
clear and important prophecies in the Bible, as an hiftorical compliment, written above an hundred and fifty years
after the death of the prophet ?——We contend, fir, that
this is a prophecy and not a hiftory ; that God called
Cyrus by his name; declared that he fhould conquer Babylon ; and defcribed the means by which he fhould do it,
above one hundred years before Cyrus was born, and
when there was no probability of fuch an event. *Porphyry*
could not refift the evidence of *Daniel's* prophecies, but by
faying, that they were forged after the events predicted had
taken place ; *Voltaire* could not refift the evidence of the
prediction of *Jefus*, concerning the deftruction of Jerufalem, but by faying that the account was written after Jerufalem had been deftroyed; and you, at length, (though for
aught I know, you may have had predeceffors in this pre-
fumption,) unable to refift the evidence of *Ifaiah's* prophecies, contend that they are bombaftical rant, without
application, though the application is circumftantial; and
deftitute of meaning, though the meaning is fo obvious
that it cannot be miftaken; and that one of them is not
a prophecy, but an hiftorical compliment written after
the event. We will not, fir, give up Daniel and St. Matthew to the impudent affertions of Porphyry and Voltaire, nor will we give up Ifaiah to your affertion. Proof,
proof is what we require, and not affertion : we will not
relinquifh our religion, in obedience to your abufive affertion refpecting the prophets of God. That the wonderful abfurdity of this hypothefis may be more obvious to
you, I beg you to confider that Cyrus was a Perfian, had
been brought up in the religion of his country, and was
probably addicted to the Magian fuperftition of two independent Beings, equal in power but different in principle, one the author of light and of all good, the other
the author of darknefs and all evil. Now is it probable

that a captive Jew, meaning to compliment the greateſt prince in the world, ſhould be ſo ſtupid as to tell the prince that his religion was a lie? "I am the Lord, and there is none elſe; I form the *light* and create *darkneſs*, I make peace and create evil; I the Lord do all theſe things."

But if you will perſevere in believing that the prophecy concerning Cyrus was written after the event, peruſe the burden of Babylon; was that alſo written after the event? Were the Medes *then* ſtirred up againſt Babylon? Was Babylon, the glory of the kingdoms, the beauty of the Chaldees, *then* overthrown, and become as Sodom and Gomorrah? Was it *then* uninhabited? Was it *then* neither fit for the Arabian's tent nor the ſhepherd's fold? Did the wild beaſts of the deſert *then* lie there? Did the wild beaſts of the iſlands *then* cry in their deſolate houſes, and dragons in their pleaſant palaces? Were Nebuchadnezzar and Belſhazzar, the ſon and the grandſon, *then* cut off? Was Babylon *then* become a poſſeſſion of the bittern, and pools of water? Was it *then* ſwept with the beſom of deſtruction, ſo ſwept that the world knows not now where to find it?

I am unwilling to attribute bad deſigns, deliberate wickedneſs, to you, or to any man; I cannot avoid believing, that you think you have truth on your ſide, and that you are doing ſervice to mankind in endeavouring to root out what you eſteem ſuperſtition. What I blame you for is this——that you have attempted to leſſen the authority of the Bible by ridicule, more than by reaſon; that you have brought forward every petty objection which your ingenuity could diſcover, or your induſtry pick up from the writings of others; and without taking any notice of the anſwers which have been repeatedly given to theſe objections, you urge and enforce them as if they were new. There is certainly ſome novelty, at leaſt in your manner, for you go beyond all others in boldneſs of aſſertion, and in profaneneſs of argumentation; Bolingbroke and Voltaire muſt yield the palm of ſcurrility to Thomas Paine.

E 3

Permit me to ftate to you, what would, in my opinion, have been a better mode of proceeding; better fuited to the character of an honeft man, fincere in his endeavours to fearch out truth. Such a man, in reading the Bible, would, in the firft place, examine whether the Bible attributed to the Supreme Being any attributes repugnant to holinefs, truth, juftice, goodnefs; whether it reprefented him as fubject to human infirmities; whether it excluded him from the government of the world, or affigned the origin of it to chance, and an eternal conflict of atoms. Finding nothing of this kind in the Bible, (for the deftruction of the Canaanites by his exprefs command, I have fhewn not to be repugnant to his moral juftice,) he would, in the fecond place, confider that the Bible being, as to many of its parts, a very old book, and written by various authors, and at different and diftant periods, there might, probably, occur fome difficulties and apparent contradictions in the hiftorical part of it; he would endeavour to remove thefe difficulties, to reconcile thefe apparent contradictions, by the rules of fuch found criticifm as he would ufe in examining the contents of any other book; and if he found that moft of them were of a trifling nature, arifing from fhort additions inferted into the text as explanatory and fupplemental, or from miftakes and omiffions of tranfcribers, he would infer that all the reft were capable of being accounted for, though he was not able to do it; and he would be the more willing to make this conceffion, from obferving, that there ran through the whole book an harmony and connection, utterly inconfiftent with every idea of forgery and deceit. He would then, in the third place, obferve, that the miraculous and hiftorical parts of this book were fo intermixed, that they could not be feparated; that they muft either both be true, or both falfe; and from finding that the hiftorical part was as well or better authenticated than that of any other hiftory, he would admit the miraculous part; and to confirm himfelf in this belief, he would advert to the prophecies; well knowing that the prediction of things to come, was as certain a proof of the divine interpofition, as the performance of a miracle could be. If he fhould find, as he certainly would, that many ancient prophecies had been fulfilled in all their circumftances, and that fome were fulfilling at this very day, he would not fuffer a few feeming or real difficulties to overbalance the weight of this accumulated evidence for the truth of the Bible. Such, I prefume to think, would be a proper conduct in all thofe who are defirous of forming a rational and impartial judgment on the fubject of revealed religion.——To return.——

As to your obfervation, that the book of Ifaiah is (at leaft in tranflation) that kind of compofition and falfe tafte, which is properly called profe run mad——I have only to remark, that your tafte for Hebrew poetry, even judging of it from tranflation, would be more correct if you would fuffer yourfelf to be informed on the fubject by Bifhop Lowth, who tells you in his *Prelections*——" that a poem tranflated literally from the Hebrew into any other language, whilft the fame forms of the fentences remain, will ftill retain, even as far as relates to verfification, much of its native dignity, and a faint appearance of verfification."' (Gregory's Tranfl.) If this is what you mean by profe run mad, your obfervation may be admitted.

You explain at fome length your notion of the mifapplication made by St. Matthew of the prophecy in Ifaiah ——" Behold, a virgin fhall conceive and bear a fon." That paffage has been handled largely and minutely by almoft every commentator, and it is too important to be handled fuperficially by any one : I am not on the prefent occafion concerned to explain it. It is quoted by you to prove, and it is the only inftance you produce——that Ifaiah was " a lying prophet and an impoftor." Now I maintain, that this very inftance proves, that he was a true prophet, and no impoftor. The hiftory of the prophecy, as delivered in the feventh chapter, is this——Rezin king of Syria, and Pekah king of Ifrael, made war upon Ahaz king of Judah; not merely, or perhaps, not at all, for the fake of plunder or the conqueft of territory, but with a declared purpofe of making an entire revolution in the government of Judah, of deftroying the royal houfe of David, and of placing another family on the throne. Their purpofe is thus expreffed——"Let us go up againft Judah, and vex it, and let us make a breach therein for us, and fet a king in the midft of it, even the fon of Tabeal."——Now what did the Lord commiffion Ifaiah to fay to Ahaz? Did he commiffion him to fay, The kings fhall not vex thee? No.——The kings fhall not conquer thee? No.——The kings fhall not fucceed againft thee?——No: ——he commiffioned him to fay, "It (the purpofe of the two kings) fhall not ftand, neither fhall it come to pafs." I demand——Did it ftand, did it come to pafs? Was any revolution effected? Was the royal houfe of David dethroned and deftroyed? Was Tabeal ever made king of Judah? No. The prophecy was perfectly accomplifhed. You fay, "Inftead of thefe two kings failing in their attempt againft Ahaz, they fucceeded; Ahaz was defeated and deftroyed."——I deny the fact; Ahaz was defeated, but not deftroyed; and even the "two hundred thoufand women, and fons, and daughters," whom you reprefent as carried into captivity: they were not carried into captivity: they were made captives, but they were not carried into captivity: for the chief men of Samaria, being admonifhed by a prophet, would not fuffer Pekah to bring the captives into the land——"They rofe up, and took the captives, and with the fpoil clothed all that were naked among them, and arrayed them, and fhod them, and gave them to eat and to drink, and anointed them, and carried all the feeble of them upon affes, (fome humanity, you fee, amongft thofe Ifraelites, whom you every where reprefent as barbarous brutes,) and brought them to Jericho, the city of palm-trees, to their brethren." 2 Chron. xxviii. 15. ——The kings did fail in their attempt; their attempt was to deftroy the houfe of David, and to make a revolution; but they made no revolution, they did not deftroy the houfe of David, for Ahaz flept with his fathers; and Hezekiah, his fon, of the houfe of David, reigned in his ftead.

LETTER VI.

AFTER what I conceive to be a great mifreprefentation of the character and conduct of Jeremiah, you bring forward an objection which Spinoza and others before you had much infifted upon, though it is an objection which neither affects the genuinenefs, nor the authenticity, of the book of Jeremiah, any more than the blunder of a bookbinder, in mifplacing the fheets of your performance, would leffen its authority. The objection is, that the book of Jeremiah has been put together in a difordered ftate. It is acknowledged, that the order of time is not every where obferved; but the caufe of the confufion is not known. Some attribute it to *Baruch* collecting into one volume all the feveral prophecies which Jeremiah had written, and neglecting to put them in their proper places:—others think that the feveral parts of the work were at firft properly arranged, but that through accident, or the careleffnefs of tranfcribers, they were deranged:—others contend, that there is no confufion; that prophecy differs from hiftory, in not being fubject to an accurate obfervance of time and order. But leaving this matter to be fettled by critical difcuffion, let us come to a matter of greater importance—to your charge againft Jeremiah for his duplicity, and for his falfe prediction. Firft, as to his duplicity:

Jeremiah, on account of his having boldly predicted the deftruction of Jerufalem, had been thruft into a miry dungeon by the princes of Judah who fought his life; there he would have perifhed, had not one of the eunuchs taken compaffion on him, and petitioned king Zedekiah in his favour, faying, " Thefe men (the princes) have done evil in all that they have done to Jeremiah the prophet, (no fmall teftimony this, of the probity of the prophet's character,) whom they have caft into the dungeon, and he is like to die for hunger."—On this reprefentation Jeremiah was taken out of the dungeon by an order from the king, who foon afterwards fent privately for him, and

defired him to conceal nothing from him, binding himfelf,
by an oath, that, whatever might be the nature of his
prophecy, he would not put him to death, or deliver him
into the hands of the princes who fought his life. Jeremiah
delivered to him the purpofe of God refpecting the fate
of Jerufalem.   The conference being ended, the king,
anxious to perform his oath, to preferve the life of the
prophet, difmiffed him, faying, " Let no man know of
thefe words, and thou fhalt not die.   But if the princes
hear that I have talked with thee, and they come unto
thee, and fay unto thee, Declare unto us now what thou
haft faid unto the king, hide it not from us, and we will
not put thee to death; alfo what the king faid unto thee :
then thou fhalt fay unto them, I prefented my fupplication before the king, that he would not caufe me to
return to Jonathan's houfe to die there.   Then came all
the princes unto Jeremiah, and afked him, and he told
them according to all thefe words that the king had commanded."——Thus, you remark, " this man of God, as
he is called, could tell a lie, or very ftrongly prevaricate;
for certainly he did not go to Zedekiah to make his fupplication, neither did he make it."——It is not faid that he
told the princes he *went* to make his fupplication, but
that he *prefented* it: now it is faid in the preceding chapter,
that he did make the fupplication, and it is probable
that in this conference he renewed it; but be that as it
may, I contend that Jeremiah was not guilty of duplicity,
or, in more intelligible terms, that he did not violate
any law of nature, or of civil fociety, in what he did on
this occafion.   He told the truth, in part, to fave his life;
and he was under no obligation to tell the whole to men
who were certainly his enemies, and no good fubjects to
his king.   " In a matter (fays Puffendorf) which I am not
obliged to declare to another, if I cannot, with fafety,
conceal the whole, I may fairly difcover no more than a
part."   Was Jeremiah under any *obligation* to declare to
the princes what had paffed in his conference with the
king ? You may as well fay, that the houfe of lords has
a right to compel privy counfellors to reveal the king's

fecrets. The king cannot juftly require a privy counfellor to tell a lie for him; but he may require him not to divulge his *counfels* to thofe who have no right to know them.——Now for the falfe prediction—I will give the defcription of it in your own words.

" In the thirty-fourth chapter is a prophecy of Jeremiah to Zedekiah, in thefe words, ver. 2:—' Thus faith the Lord, Behold, I will give this city into the hands of the king of Babylon, and will burn it with fire; and thou fhalt not efcape out of his hand, but thou fhalt furely be taken, and delivered into his hand; and thine eyes fhall behold the eyes of the king of Babylon, and he fhall fpeak with thee mouth to mouth, and thou fhalt go to Babylon. *Yet hear the word of the Lord, O Zedekiah king of Judah; thus faith the Lord, Thou fhalt not die by the fword, but thou fhalt die in peace; and with the burnings of thy fathers, the former kings that were before thee, fo fhall they burn odours for thee, and will lament thee, faying, Ah, lord! for I have pronounced the word, faith the Lord.'*

" Now, inftead of Zedekiah beholding the eyes of the king of Babylon, and fpeaking with him mouth to mouth, and dying in peace, and with the burnings of odours, as at the funeral of his fathers (as Jeremiah had declared the Lord himfelf had pronounced) the reverfe, according to the 52d chapter, was the cafe; it is there ftated, verfe 10, ' That the king of Babylon flew the fons of Zedekiah before his eyes; that he put out the eyes of Zedekiah, and bound him in chains, and carried him to Babylon, and put him prifon till the day of his death. What can we fay of thefe prophets, but that they are impoftors and liars?" I can fay this——that the prophecy you have produced, was fulfilled in all its parts; and what then fhall be faid of thofe who call Jeremiah a liar and an impoftor? Here then we are fairly at iffue——you affirm that the prophecy was not fulfilled, and I affirm that it was fulfilled in all its parts. "I will give this city into the hands of the king of Babylon, and he fhall burn it with fire:" fo fays the prophet; what fays the hiftory? "They (the forces of the king of Babylon) burnt the houfe of God, and brake down the walls of Jerufalem, and burnt all the palaces thereof with fire." (2 Chron. xxxvi. 19.)—— " Thou fhalt not efcape out of his hand, but fhalt furely be *taken* and *delivered* into his hand:" fo fays the prophet; what fays the hiftory? " The men of war fled by night, and the king went the way towards the plain, and the army of the Chaldees purfued after the king, and overtook him in the plains of Jericho; and all his army were fcattered from him; fo they *took* the king, and *brought him up to the king of Babylon*, to Riblah." (2 Kings xxv. 5.) ——The prophet goes on, " Thine eyes fhall behold the eyes of the king of Babylon, and he fhall fpeak with thee mouth to mouth." No pleafant circumftance this to Zedekiah, who had provoked the king of Babylon, by revolting from him! The hiftory fays, " The king of Babylon gave judgment upon Zedekiah," or as it is more literally rendered from the Hebrew, " *fpake judgments with him* at Riblah."——The prophet concludes this part with, " And thou fhalt go to Babylon:" the hiftory fays, " The king of Babylon bound him in chains, and carried him to Babylon, and put him in prifon till the day of his death." (Jer. lii. 11.)—" Thou fhalt not die by the fword." He did not die by the fword, he *did not fall in* battle.——" But thou fhalt die in peace." He did die in peace, he neither expired on the rack, nor on the fcaffold; was neither ftrangled nor poifoned; no unufual fate of captive kings! he died peaceably in his bed, though that bed was in a prifon.——" And with the burnings of thy fathers fhall they burn odours for thee." I cannot prove from the hiftory that this part of the prophecy was accomplifhed, nor can you prove that it was not. The probability is, that it was accomplifhed; and I have two reafons on which I ground this probability.—Daniel, Shadrach, Mefhach, and Abednego, to fay nothing of other Jews, were men of great authority in the court of the king of Babylon, before and after the commencement of the imprifonment of Zedekiah; and Daniel continued in power till the fubverfion of the kingdom of Babylon by Cyrus.——Now it feems to me to be very probable, that

Daniel, and the other great men of the Jews, would both have inclination to requeſt, and influence enough with the king of Babylon to obtain permiſſion to bury their deceaſed prince Zedekiah, after the manner of his fathers.——But if there had been no Jews at Babylon of confequence enough to make ſuch a requeſt, ſtill it is probable that the king of Babylon would have ordered the Jews to bury and lament their departed prince, after the manner of their country. Monarchs, like other men, are confcious of the inſtability of human condition; and when the pomp of war has ceaſed, when the inſolence of conqueſt is abated, and the fury of refentment fubfided, they feldom fail to revere royalty even in its ruins, and grant without reluctance proper obſequies to the remains of captive kings.

You profeſs to have been particular in treating of the books aſcribed to Iſaiah and Jeremiah.——Particular! in what? You have particularized two or three paſſages, which you have endeavoured to repreſent as objectionable, and which I hope have been ſhewn, to the reader's fatiſfaction, to be not juſtly liable to your cenfure; and you have paſſed over all the other parts of theſe books without notice. Had you been particular in your examination, you would have found cauſe to admire the probity and the intrepidity of the characters of the authors of them; you would have met with many inſtances of ſublime compofition, and what is of more confequence, with many inſtances of prophetical veracity:——particularities of theſe kinds you have wholly overlooked. I cannot account for this; I have no right, no inclination, to call you a dishoneſt man: am I juſtified in confidering you as a man not altogether deſtitute of ingenuity, but ſo entirely under the dominion of prejudice in every thing refpecting the Bible, that, like a corrupted judge previouſly determined to give fentence on one fide, you are negligent in the examination of truth?

You proceed to the reſt of the prophets, and you take them collectively, carefully however, ſelecting for your obſervations ſuch particularities as are beſt calculated to render, if poſſible, the prophets odious or ridiculous in the

F

eyes of your readers. You confound prophets with poets
and muficians: I would diftinguifh them thus: many prophets were poets and muficians, but all poets and muficians were not prophets. Prophecies were often delivered
in poetic language and meafure; but flights and meta-
phors of the Jewifh poets, have not, as you affirm, been
foolifhly erected into what are now called prophecies——
they are now called, and have always been called, prophecies—becaufe they were real predictions, fome of
which have received, fome are now receiving, and all will
receive, their full accomplifhment.

That there were falfe prophets, witches, necromancers,
conjurers, fortune-tellers, among the Jews, no perfon will
attempt to deny; no nation, barbarous or civilized, has
been without them: but when you would degrade the
prophets of the Old Teftament to a level with thefe conjuring, dreaming, ftrolling, gentry—when you would reprefent them as fpending their lives in fortune-telling,
cafting nativities, predicting riches, fortunate or unfortu-
nate marriages, conjuring for loft goods, &c. I muft be
allowed to fay, that you wholly miftake their office, and
mifreprefent their character: their office was to convey to
the children of Ifrael the commands, the promifes, the
threatenings of Almighty God: and their character was
that of men fuftaining, with fortitude, perfecution in the
difcharge of their duty. There were falfe prophets in
abundance amongft the Jews; and if you oppofe thefe to
the true prophets, and call them both party prophets, you
have the liberty of doing fo, but you will not thereby confound the diftinction between truth and falfehood. Falfe
prophets are fpoken of with deteftation in many parts of
fcripture; particularly by Jeremiah, who accufes them of
prophefying lies in the name of the Lòrd, faying, "I have
dreamed, I have dreamed:—Behold, I am againft the prophets, faith the Lord, that ufe their tongues, and fay, He
faith; that prophefy falfe dreams, and caufe my people to
err by their lies, and by their lightnefs." Jeremiah cau-
tions his countrymen againft giving credit to their prophets, to their diviners, to their dreamers, to their en-

chanters, to their forcerers, " which fpeak unto you, faying, Ye fhall not ferve the king of Babylon." You cannot
think more contemptibly of thefe gentry, than they were
thought of by the true prophets at the time they lived;
but, as Jeremiah fays on this fubject, "what is the chaff to
the wheat?" what are the falfe prophets fo the true ones?
Every thing good is liable to abufe; but who argues
againft the ufe of a thing from the abufe of it? againft
phyficians, becaufe there are pretenders to phyfic? Was
Ifaiah a fortune-teller, predicting riches, when he faid to
king Hezekiah, "Behold the days come, that all that is in
thine houfe, and that which thy fathers have laid up in
ftore until this day, fhall be carried to Babylon: nothing
fhall be left, faith the Lord. And of thy fons that fhall
iffue from thee, which thou fhalt beget, fhall they take
away, and they fhall be eunuchs in the palace of the king
of Babylon." Fortune-tellers generally predict good luck
to their fimple cuftomers, that they may make fomething
by their trade; but Ifaiah predicts to a monarch, defolation of his country, and ruin of his family. This prophecy
was fpoken in the year before Chrift 713; and, above
an hundred years afterwards, it was accomplifhed; when
Nebuchadnezzar took Jerufalem, and carried out thence
all the treafures of the houfe of the Lord, and the treafures of the king's houfe, (2 Kings xxiv. 13.) and when he
commanded the mafter of his eunuchs, (Dan. i. 3.) that he
fhould take certain of the children of Ifrael, and of the
king's feed, and of the princes, and educate them for three
years, till they were able to ftand before the king.

Jehoram king of Ifrael, Jehofhaphat king of Judah,
and the king of Edom, going with their armies to make
war on the king of Moab, came into a place where there
was no water either for their men or cattle. In this dif-
trefs they waited upon Elifha, (an high honour for one
of your conjurers,) by the advice of Jehofhaphat, who
knew that the word of the Lord was with him. The
prophet, on feeing Jehoram, an idolatrous prince, who
had revolted from the worfhip of the true God, come to
confult him, faid to him,——" Get thee to the prophets

of thy father and the prophets of thy mother."——This you think ſhews Eliſha to have been a party prophet, full of venom and vulgarity——it ſhews him to have been a man of great courage, who reſpected the dignity of his own character, the ſacredneſs of his office as a prophet of God, whoſe duty it was to reprove the wickedneſs of kings, as of other men. He ordered them to make the valley where they were full of ditches:——this, you ſay, " every countryman could have told, that the way to get water was to dig for it:"——but this is not a true repreſentation of the caſe; the ditches were not dug that water might be gotten by digging for it, but that they might hold the water when it ſhould miraculouſly come, " without wind or rain," from another country; and it did come " from the way of Edom, and the country was filled with water."——As to Eliſha's curſing the little children who had mocked him, and their deſtruction in conſequence of his imprecation, the whole ſtory muſt be taken together. The provocation he received is, by ſome, conſidered as an inſult offered to him, not as a man but as a prophet, and that the perſons who offered it were not what we underſtand by little children, but grown-up youths; the term child being applied, in the Hebrew language, to grown-up perſons. Be this as it may, the curſing was the act of the prophet; had it been a ſin it would not have been followed by a miraculous deſtruction of the offenders; for this was the act of God, who beſt knows who deſerves puniſhment. What effect ſuch a ſignal judgment had on the idolatrous inhabitants of the land, is no where ſaid; but it is probable it was not without a good effect.

Ezekiel and Daniel lived during the Babylonian captivity; you allow their writings to be genuine. In this you differ from ſome of the greateſt adverſaries of Chriſtianity; and in my opinion cut up, by this conceſſion, the very root of your whole performance. It is next to an impoſſibility for any man, who admits the book of Daniel to be a genuine book, and who examines that book with intelligence and impartiality, to refuſe his aſſent to the truth of

Chriftianity. As to your faying, that the interpretations, which commentators and priefts have made of thefe books, only fhew the fraud, or the extreme folly, to which credulity and prieftcraft can go: I confider it as nothing but a proof of the extreme folly or fraud to which prejudice and infidelity can carry a minute philofopher. You profefs a fondnefs for fcience; I will refer you to a fcientific man, who was neither a commentator nor a prieft,——to Fergufon——In a tract entitled——The Year of our Saviour's Crucifixion afcertained; and the darknefs, at the time of his crucifixion, proved to be fupernatural——this real philofopher interprets the remarkable prophecy in the 9th chapter of Daniel, and concludes his differtation in the following words——" Thus we have an aftronomical demonftration of the truth of this ancient prophecy, feeing that the prophetic year of the Meffiah's being cut off, was the very fame with the aftronomical." I have fomewhere read an account of a folemn difputation which was held at Venice, in the laft century, between a Jew and a Chriftian;——the Chriftian ftrongly argued from Daniel's prophecy of the feventy weeks, that Jefus was the Meffiah whom the Jews had long expected, from the predictions of their prophets;——the learned Rabbi, who prefided at this difputation, was fo forcibly ftruck by the argument, that he put an end to the bufinefs, by faying,——" Let us fhut up our Bibles; for if we proceed in the examination of this prophecy, it will make us all become Chriftians." Was it a fimilar apprehenfion which deterred you from fo much as opening the book of Daniel? You have not produced from it one exceptionable paffage. I hope you will read that book with attention, with intelligence, and with an unbiaffed mind follow the advice of our Saviour when he quoted this very prophecy——" Let him that readeth underftand"—— and I fhall not defpair of your converfion from deifm to Chriftianity.

In order to difcredit the authority of the books which you allow to be genuine, you form a ftrange and prodigious hypothefis concerning Ezekiel and Daniel, for which there is no manner of foundation either in hiftory or pro-

bability. You fuppofe thefe two men to have had no
dreams, no vifions, no revelation from God Almighty;
but to have pretended to thefe things; and, under that
difguife, to have carried on an enigmatical correfpondence
relative to the recovery of their country from the Babylonian yoke. That any man in his fenfes fhould frame or
adopt fuch an hypothefis, fhould have fo little regard to
his own reputation as an impartial enquirer after truth, fo
little refpect for the underftanding of his readers, as to
obtrude it on the world, would have appeared an incredible circumftance, had not you made it a fact.

You quote a paffage from Ezekiel; in the 29th chapter,
ver. 11, fpeaking of Egypt, it is faid——" No foot of man
fhall pafs through it, nor foot of beaft fhall pafs through
it; neither fhall it be inhabited forty years:"——this, you
fay, " never came to pafs, and confequently it is falfe, as
all the books I have already reviewed are." Now that
this did come to pafs, we have, as Bifhop Newton obferves,
" the teftimonies of Megafthenes and Berofus, two heathen
hiftorians, who lived about 300 years before Chrift; one of
whom affirms, exprefsly, that Nebuchadnezzar conquered
the greater part of Africa; and the other affirms it, in effect, in faying, that when Nebuchadnezzar heard of the
death of his father, having fettled his affairs *in Egypt*, and
committed the *captives* whom he took in Egypt, to the
care of fome of his friends to bring them after him, he
hafted directly to Babylon." And if we had been poffeffed
of no teftimony in fupport of the prophecy, it would have
been an hafty conclufion, that the prophecy never came to
pafs. The hiftory of Egypt at fo remote a period, being
no where accurately and circumftantially related, I admit
that no period can be pointed out, from the age of Ezekiel
to the prefent, in which there was no foot of man or beaft
to be feen for forty years in all Egypt; but fome think that
only a part of Egypt is here fpoken of; and furely you do
not expect a literal accomplifhment of an hyperbolical expreffion, denoting great defolation; importing that the
trade of Egypt, which was carried on then, as at prefent,
by caravans, by the foot of man and beaft, fhould be anni-

hilated. Had you taken the trouble to have looked a little farther into the book from which you have made your quotation, you would have there feen a prophecy delivered above two thoufand years ago, and which has been fulfilling from that time to this——" Egypt fhall be the bafeft of the kingdoms, neither fhall it exalt itfelf any more above the nations——there fhall be no more a prince of the land of Egypt."——This you may call a dream, a vifion, a lie; I efteem it a wonderful prophecy; for " as is the prophecy, fo has been the event. Egypt was conquered by the Babylonians; and after the Babylonians by the Perfians; and after the Perfians it became fubject to the Macedonians; and after the Macedonians to the Romans; and after the Romans to the Saracens; and then to the Mamelukes; and is now a province of the Turkifh empire."

Suffer me to produce to you from this author not an enigmatical letter to Daniel refpecting the recovery of *Jerufalem,* from the hands of the king of Babylon, but an enigmatical prophecy concerning Zedekiah the king of Jerufalem, before it was taken by the Chaldeans.——" I will bring him (Zedekiah) to Babylon, to the land of the Chaldeans; yet fhall he not fee it, though he fhall die there."——How! not fee Babylon, when he fhall die there! How, moreover, is this confiftent, you may afk, with what Jeremiah had foretold——that Zedekiah fhould fee the eyes of the king of Babylon?——This darknefs of expreffion, and apparent contradiction between the two prophets, induced Zedekiah (as Jofephus informs us) to give no credit to either of them: yet he unhappily experienced, and the fact is worthy your obfervation, the truth of them both. He faw the eyes of the king of Babylon, not at Babylon, but at Riblah; his eyes were there put out; and he was carried to Babylon, yet he faw it not; and thus were the predictions of both the prophets verified, and the enigma of Ezekiel explained.

As to your wonderful difcovery that the prophecy of Jonah is a book of fome gentile, " and that it has been written as a fable, to expofe the nonfenfe, and to fatirife the vicious and malignant character of a Bible prophet, or a predicting prieft," I fhall put it, covered with *hellebore,* for the fervice of its author, on the fame fhelf with your hypothefis concerning the confpiracy of Daniel and Eze- kiel, and fhall not fay another word about it.

You conclude your objections to the Old Teftament in a triumphant ftyle; an angry opponent would fay, in a ftyle of extreme arrogance, and fottifh felf-fufficiency—— " I have gone," you fay, " through the Bible (miftaking here, as in other places, the Old Teftament for the Bible) as a man would go through a wood, with an axe on his fhoulders, and fell trees; here they lie; and the priefts if they can may replant them. They may, perhaps, ftick them in the ground, but they will never grow."——And is it poffible that you fhould think fo highly of your perform- ance, as to believe, that you have thereby demolifhed the authority of a book, which Newton himfelf efteemed the moft authentic of all hiftories; which, by its celeftial light, illumines the darkeft ages of antiquity; which is the touch- ftone whereby we are enabled to diftinguifh between true and fabulous theology, between the God of Ifrael, holy, juft, and good, and the impure rabble of heathen Baalim; which has been thought, by competent judges, to have afforded matter for the laws of Solon, and a foundation for the philofophy of Plato; which has been illuftrated by the labour of learning, in all ages and countries; and been admired and venerated for its piety, its fublimity, its vera- city, by all who were able to read and underftand it ? No, Sir; you have gone indeed through the wood, with the beft intention in the world to cut it down; but you have merely bufied yourfelf in expofing to vulgar contempt a few unfightly fhrubs, which good men had wifely concealed from public veiw; you have entangled yourfelf in thickets of thorns and briars; you have loft your way on the moun- tains of Lebanon; the goodly cedar trees whereof, lament- ing the madnefs, and pitying the blindnefs of your rage againft them, have fcorned the blunt edge and the bafe temper of your axe, and laughed unhurt at the feeblenefs of your ftroke.

In plain language, you have gone through the Old

Teſtament hunting after difficulties, and you have found
ſome real ones; theſe you have endeavoured to magnify
into inſurmountable objections to the authority of the whole
book. When it is confidered that the Old Teſtament is
compofed of feveral books, written by different authors,
and at different periods, from Mofes to Malachi, com-
prifing an abſtracted hiſtory of a particular nation for
above a thouſand years, I think the real difficulties which
occur in it are much fewer, and of much lefs importance,
than could reafonably have been expected. Apparent
difficulties you have reprefented as real ones, without
hinting at the manner in which they have been explained.
You have ridiculed things held moſt facred, and calumniated characters eſteemed moſt venerable; you have ex-
cited the fcoffs of the profane; increafed the fcepticiſm
of the doubtful; ſhaken the faith of the unlearned;
fuggeſted cavils to the " difputers of this world;" and
perplexed the minds of honeſt men who wiſh to worſhip
the God of their fathers in ſincerity and truth.——This
and more you have done in going through the Old Teſtament; but you have not fo much as glanced at the great
defign of the whole, at the harmony and mutual depend-
ence of the feveral parts. You have faid nothing of the
wifdom of God in felecting a particular people from the
reſt of mankind, not for their own fakes, but that they
might witnefs to the whole world, in fucceſſive ages, his
exiſtence and attributes; that they might be an inſtrument
of fubverting idolatry, of declaring the name of the God
of Ifrael throughout the whole earth. It was through
this nation that the Egyptians faw the wonders of God;
that the Canaanites (whom wickednefs had made a re-
proach to human nature) felt his judgments; that the
Babylonians iffued their decrees——" That none ſhould
dare to fpeak amifs of the God of Ifrael——that all ſhould
fear and tremble before him"——and it is through them
that you and I, and all the world, are not at this day wor-
ſhippers of idols. You have faid nothing of the goodnefs
of God in promiſing, that, through the feed of Abraham,
all the nations of the earth were to be bleſſed; that the

defire of all nations, the bleffing of Abraham to the gentiles, fhould come. You have paffed by all the prophecies
refpecting the coming of the Meffiah; though they abfolutely fixed the time of his coming, and of his being cut
off; defcribed his office, character, condition, fufferings,
and death, in fo circumftantial a manner, that we cannot
but be aftonifhed at the accuracy of their completion in
the perfon of Jefus of Nazareth. You have neglected
noticing the teftimony of the whole Jewifh nation to the
truth both of the natural and miraculous facts recorded
in the Old Teftament. That we may better judge of the
weight of this teftimony, let us fuppofe that God fhould
now manifeft himfelf to us, as we contend he did to the
Ifraelites in Egypt, in the defert, and in the land of Canaan; and that he fhould continue thefe manifeftations
of himfelf to our pofterity for a thoufand years or more,
punifhing or rewarding them according as they difobeyed
or obeyed his commands; what would you expect fhould be
the iffue? You would expect that our pofterity would,
in the remoteft period of time, adhere to their God, and
maintain againft all opponents the truth of the books in
which the difpenfations of God to us and to our fucceffors
had been recorded. They would not yield to the objections of men, who, not having experienced the fame
divine government, fhould, for want of fuch experience,
refufe affent to their teftimony. No; they would be to the
then furrounding nations, what the Jews are to us, witneffes of the exiftence and of the moral government of
God.

LETTER VII.

" The New Teftament, they tell us, is founded upon
the prophecies of the Old; if fo, it muft follow the fate
of its foundation."——Thus you open your attack upon

the New Teftament ; and I agree with you, that the New Teftament muft follow the fate of the Old; and that fate is to remain unimpaired by fuch efforts as you have made againft it. The New Teftament, however, is not founded folely on the prophecies of the Old. If an heathen from *Athens* or *Rome*, who had never heard of the prophecies of the Old Teftament, had been an eye-witnefs of the miracles of Jefus, he would have made the fame conclufion that the Jew Nicodemus did——" Rabbi, we know that thou art a teacher come from God ; for no man can do thefe miracles that thou doeft, except God be with him."——Our Saviour tells the Jews— " Had ye believed Mofes, ye would have believed me ; for he wrote of me"— and he bids them fearch the Scriptures; for they teftified of him ; — but, notwithftanding this appeal to the prophecies of the Old Teftament, Jefus faid to the Jews, " Though ye believe not me, believe the works"— " believe me for the very works' fake"——" if I had not done among them the works which none other man did, they had not had fin."—Thefe are fufficient proofs that the truth of Chrift's miffion was not even to the Jews, much lefs to the Gentiles, founded folely on the truth of the prophecies of the Old Teftament. So that if you could prove fome of thefe prophecies to have been mis-applied, and not completed in the perfon of Jefus, the truth of the Chriftian religion would not thereby be over-turned.—That Jefus of Nazareth was the perfon, in whom all the prophecies, direct and typical, in the Old Tefta-ment, refpecting the Meffiah, were fulfilled, is a pro-pofition founded on thofe prophecies, and to be proved by comparing them with the hiftory of his life. That Jefus was *a* prophet fent from God, is one propofition— that Jefus was *the* prophet, the Meffiah, is another : and though he certainly was both *a* prophet and *the* prophet, yet the foundations of the proof of thefe propofitions are feparate and diftinct.

The " mere exiftence of fuch a woman as Mary, and of fuch a man as Jofeph, and Jefus, is," you fay, " a matter of indifference, about which there is no ground

either to believe or to difbelieve."——Belief is different from
knowledge, with which you here feem to confound it. We
know that the whole is greater than its part——and we
know that all the angles in the fame fegment of a circle
are equal to each other——we have intuition and demonftration as grounds of this knowledge; but is there no
ground for belief of paft or future exiftence? Is there no
ground for believing that the fun will exift to-morrow, and
that your father exifted before you? You condefcend,
however, to think it probable, that there were fuch perfons
as Mary, Jofeph, and Jefus; and, without troubling yourfelf about their exiftence or non-exiftence, affuming, as it
were, for the fake of argument, but without pofitively
granting, their exiftence, you proceed to inform us, " that
it is the fable of Jefus Chrift, as told in the New Teftament,
and the wild and vifionary doctrine raifed thereon," againft
which you contend. You will not repute it a fable, that
there was fuch a man as Jefus Chrift; that he lived in
Judea near eighteen hundred years ago; that he went
about doing good, and preaching, not only in the villages
of Galilee, but in the city of Jerufalem; that he had feveral
followers who conftantly attended him; that he was put
to death by Pontius Pilate; that his difciples were numerous a few years after his death, not only in Judea, but
in Rome the capital of the world, and in every province
of the Roman empire; that a particular day has been
obferved in a religious manner by all his followers, in commemoration of a real or fuppofed refurrection; and that
the conftant celebration of baptifm, and of the Lord's
fupper, may be traced back from the prefent time to him,
as the author of thofe inftitutions. Thefe things conftitute,
I fuppofe, no part of your fable; and if thefe things be
facts, they will, when maturely confidered, draw after
them fo many other things related in the New Teftament
concerning Jefus, that there will be left for your fable but
very fcanty materials, which will require great fertility of
invention before you will drefs them up into any form
which will not difguft even a fuperficial obferver.

The miraculous conception you efteem a fable, and in

your mind it is an obfcene fable.——Impure indeed muft
that man's imagination be, who can difcover any obfcenity
in the angel's declaration to Mary——" The Holy Ghoft
fhall come upon thee, and the power of the Higheft fhall
overfhadow thee: therefore that Holy thing which fhall
be born of thee fhall be called the Son of God."—I wonder
you do not find obfcenity in Genefis, where it is faid,
" The Spirit of God moved upon the face of the waters,"
and brought order out of confufion, a world out of a chaos,
by his foftering influence. As to the Chriftian faith being
built upon the heathen mythology, there is no ground
whatever for the affertion; there would have been fome
for faying, that much of the heathen mythology was built
upon the events recorded in the Old Teftament.

You come now to a demonftration, or, which amounts
to the fame thing, to a propofition which cannot, you fay,
be controverted :——firft, " That the *agreement* of all the
parts of a ftory does not prove that ftory to be true, becaufe the parts may agree and the whole may be falfe ;——
fecondly, that the *difagreement* of the parts of a ftory
proves that the *whole cannot be true.* The agreement does
not prove truth, but the difagreement proves falfehood
pofitively." Great ufe, I perceive, is to be made of this
propofition. You will pardon my unfkilfulnefs in dialectics,
if I prefume to controvert the truth of this abftract propofition, as applied to any purpofe in life. The agreement
of the parts of a ftory implies that the ftory has been
told by, at leaft, two perfons) the life of Doctor Johnfon,
for inftance, by Sir John Hawkins and Mr. Bofwell. Now
I think it fcarcely poffible for even two perfons, and the
difficulty is increafed if there are more than two, to write
the hiftory of the life of any one of their acquaintance,
without there being a confiderable difference between them,
with refpect to the number and order of the incidents of
his life. Some things will be omitted by one, and mentioned by the other; fome things will be briefly touched
by one, and the fame things will be circumftantially de-
tailed by the other; the fame things, which are mentioned
in the fame way by them both, may not be mentioned as

having happened exactly at the fame point of time; with other poffible and probable differences. But thefe real or apparent difficulties, in minute circumftances, will not invalidate their teftimony as to the material tranfactions of his life, much lefs will they render the whole of it a fable. If feveral independent witneffes, of fair character, fhould agree in all the parts of a ftory, (in teftifying, for inftance, that a murder or a robbery was committed at a particular time, in a particular place, and by a certain individual,) every court of juftice in the world would admit the fact, notwithftanding the abftract poffibility of the whole being falfe :—again, if feveral honeft men fhould agree in faying, that they faw the king of France beheaded, though they fhould difagree as to the figure of the guil-lotine, or the fize of his executioner, as to the king's hands being bound or loofe, as to his being compofed or agitated in afcending the fcaffold, yet every court of juftice in the world would think, that fuch difference, refpecting the circumftances of the fact, did not invalidate the evidence refpecting the fact itfelf. When you fpeak of the whole of a ftory, you cannot mean every particular circumftance connected with the ftory, but not effential to it; you muft mean the pith and marrow of the ftory; for it would be impoffible to eftablifh the truth of any fact, (of Admirals Byng or Keppel, for example, having neglected or not neglected their duty,) if a difagreement in the evidence of witneffes, in minute points, fhould be confidered as an-nihilating the weight of their evidence in points of impor-tance. In a word, the relation of a fact differs effentially from the demonftration of a theorem. If one ftep is left out, one link in the chain of ideas conftituting a demon-ftration is omitted, theconclufion will be deftroyed ; but a fact may be eftablifhed, notwithftanding a difagreement of the witneffes in certain trifling particulars of their evidence refpecting it.

You apply your incontrovertible propofition to the genealogies of Chrift given by Matthew and Luke—there is a difagreement between them ; therefore, you fay, " If Matthew fpeak truth, Luke fpeaks falfehood ; and if Luke

fpeak truth, Matthew fpeaks falfehood : and thence there
is no authority for believing either ; and if they cannot be
believed even in the very firft thing they fay and fet out to
prove, they are not entitled to be believed in any thing they
fay afterwards." I cannot admit either your premifes or
your conclufion ;—not your conclufion ; becaufe two
authors, who differ in tracing back the pedigree of an individual for above a thoufand years, cannot, on that account, be efteemed incompetent to bear teftimony to the
tranfactions of his life, unlefs an intention to falfify could
be proved againft them. If two Welfh hiftorians fhould at
this time write the life of any remarkable man of their
country, who had been dead twenty or thirty years, and
fhould, through different branches of their genealogical
tree, carry up their pedigree to *Cadwallon,* would they, on
account of that difference, be difcredited in every thing
they faid ? Might it not be believed that they gave the
pedigree as they had found it recorded in different inftru-
ments, but without the leaft intention to write a falfehood ?—I cannot admit your premifes ; becaufe Matthew
fpeaks truth, and Luke fpeaks truth, though they do not
fpeak the fame truth ; Matthew giving the genealogy of
Jofeph the reputed father of Jefus, and Luke giving the
genealogy of Mary the real mother of Jefus. If you will
not admit this, other explanations of the difficulty might
be given ; but I hold it fufficient to fay, that the authors
had no defign to deceive the reader, that they took their
accounts from the public regifters, which were carefully
kept, and that had they been fabricators of thefe genealogies, they would have been expofed at the time to inftant
detection ; and the certainty of that detection would have
prevented them from making the attempt to impofe a falfe
genealogy on the Jewifh nation.

But that you may effectually overthrow the credit of
thefe genealogies, you make the following calculation :—
" From the birth of David to the birth of Chrift is upwards
of 1080 years ; and as there were but 27 full generations,
to find the average age of each perfon mentioned in
St. Matthew's lift at the time his firft fon was born, it is
only neceffary to divide 1080 by 27, which gives 40 years

for each perfon. As the life-time of man was then but of
the fame extent it is now, it is an abfurdity to fuppofe,
that 27 generations fhould all be old batchelors, before
they married. So far from this genealogy being a folemn
truth, it is not even a reafonable lie."——This argument
affumes the appearance of arithmetical accuracy, and the
conclufion is in a ftyle which even its truth would not excufe:——yet the argument is good for nothing, and the conclufion is not true. You have read the Bible with fome
attention; and you are extremely liberal in imputing to it
lies and abfurdities; read it over again, efpecially the
books of the Chronicles, and you will there find, that in
the genealogical lift of St. Matthew, three generations are
omitted between Joram and Ozias; Joram was the father
of Azariah, Azariah of Joafh, Joafh of Amaziah, and Amaziah of Ozias.——I inquire not, in this place, whence this
omiffion proceeded; whether it is to be attributed to an
error in the genealogical tables from whence Matthew took
his account, or to a corruption of the text of the evangelift: ftill it is an omiffion. Now if you will add thefe three
generations to the 27 you mention, and divide 1080 by
30, you will find the average age when thefe Jews had
each of them their firft fon born was 36. They married
fooner than they ought to have done, according to Ariftotle, who fixes thirty-feven as the moft proper age, when
a man fhould marry. Nor was it neceffary that they
fhould have been old batchelors, though each of them had
not a fon to fucceed him till he was thirty-fix; they might
have been married at twenty, without having a fon till
they were forty. You affume in your argument, that the
firft-born fon fucceeded the father in the lift——this is not
true. Solomon fucceeded David; yet David had at leaft
fix fons, who were grown to manhood before Solomon
was born; and Rehoboam had at leaft three fons before
he had Abia (Abijah) who fucceeded him.——It is needlefs to
cite more inftances to this purpofe; but from thefe, and
other circumftances which might be infifted upon, I can
fee no ground for believing, that the genealogy of Jefus
Chrift, mentioned by St. Matthew, is not a folemn truth.

You infift much upon fome things being mentioned by

one evangelift, which are not mentioned by all or by any of the others: and you take this to be à reafon why we fhould confider the gofpels, not as the works of Matthew, Mark, Luke, and John, but as the productions of fome *unconnected* individuals, each of whom made his own legend. I do not admit the truth of this fuppofition; but I may be allowed to ufe it as an argument againft yourfelf—it removes every poffible fufpicion of fraud and impofture, and confirms the gofpel hiftory in the ftrongeft manner. Four *unconnected* individuals have each written memoirs of the life of Jefus; from whatever fource they derived their materials, it is evident that they agree in a great many particulars of the laft importance; fuch as the purity of his manners; the fanctity of his doctrines; the multitude and publicity of his miracles; the perfecuting fpirit of his enemies; the manner of his death and the certainty of his refurrection: and whilft they agree in thefe great points, their difagreement in points of little confequence is rather a confirmation of the truth, than an indication of the falfehood, of their feveral accounts.—Had they agreed in nothing, their teftimony ought to have been rejected as a legendary tale; had they agreed in every thing, it might have been fufpected, that, inftead of unconnected individuals, they were a fet of impoftors. The manner in which the evangelifts have recorded the particulars of the life of Jefus, is wholly conformable to what we experience in other biographers, and claims our higheft affent to its truth; notwithftanding the force of your incontrovertible propofition.

As an inftance of contradiction between the evangelifts, you tell us, that Matthew fays, the angel announcing the immaculate conception appeared unto Jofeph; but Luke fays, he appeared unto Mary.—The angel, Sir, appeared unto them both; to Mary when he informed her that fhe fhould, by the power of God, conceive a fon; to Jofeph, fome months afterwards, when Mary's pregnancy was vifible; in the interim fhe had paid a vifit of three months to her coufin Elifabeth. It might have been expected, that from the accuracy with which you have read your Bible, you could not have confounded thefe obvioufly diftinct appearances; but men, even of candour, are liable to miftakes. Who, you afk, would now believe a girl, who fhould fay fhe was gotten with child by a ghoft?——who, but yourfelf, would ever have afked a queftion fo abominably indecent and profane? I cannot argue with you on this fubject.——You will never perfuade the world, that the Holy Spirit of God has any refemblance to the ftage ghofts in Hamlet or Macbeth, from which you feem to have derived your idea of it.

The ftory of the maffacre of the young children by the order of Herod, is mentioned only by Matthew; and therefore you think it is a lie. We muft give up all hiftory if we refufe to admit facts recorded by only one hiftorian. Matthew addreffed his gofpél to the Jews, and put them in mind of a circumftance, of which they muft have had a melancholy remembrance; but gentile converts were lefs interefted in that event. The evangelifts were not writing the life of Herod, but of Jefus; it is no wonder that they omitted, above half a century after the death of Herod, an inftance of his cruelty, which was not effentially con-nected with their fubject. The maffacre, however, was probably known even at Rome; and it was certainly cor-refpondent to the character of Herod. John, you fay, at the time of the maffacre, " was under two years of age, and yet he efcaped; fo that the ftory circumftantially be-lies itfelf."—John was fix months older than Jefus: and you cannot prove that he was not beyond the age to which the order of Herod extended; it probably reached no farther than to thofe who had completed their firft year, without including thofe who had entered upon their fecond : but without infifting upon this, ftill I contend that you cannot prove John to have been under two years of age at the time of the maffacre; and I could give many probable reafons to the contrary. Nor is it certain that John was, at that time, in that part of the country to which the edict of Herod extended. But there would be no end of anfwering, at length, all your little objections.

No two of the evangelifts, you obferve, agree in re-citing, *exactly in the fame words*, the written infcription

which was put over Chrift when he was crucified.——I
admit that there is an uneffential verbal difference; and
are you certain that there was not a verbal difference in the
infcriptions themfelves?——One was written in Hebrew,
another in Greek, another in Latin; and though they had
all the fame meaning, yet it is probable, that, if two men
had tranflated the Hebrew and the Latin into Greek, there
would have been a verbal difference between their tranf-
lations. You have rendered yourfelf famous by writing
a book called——The Rights of Man:——had you been
guillotined by Robefpierre, with this title, written in French,
Englifh, and German, and affixed to the guillotine—Thomas
Paine, of America, author of the Rights of Man——and
had four perfons, fome of whom had feen the execution,
and the reft had heard of it from eye-witneffes, written
fhort accounts of your life twenty years or more after your
death, and one had faid the infcription was——This is
Thomas Paine, the author of The Rights of Man—another,
The author of The Rights of Man——a third, This is the
author of The Rights of Man——and a fourth, Thomas
Paine, of America, the author of The Rights of Man——
would any man of common fenfe have doubted, on account
of this difagreement, the veracity of the authors in writing
your life?——" The only one," you tell us, " of the men
called apoftles, who appears to have been near the fpot
where Jefus was crucified, was Peter."——This your affertion is not true——we do not know that Peter was prefent
at the crucifixion; but we do know that John, the difciple
whom Jefus loved, was prefent; for Jefus fpoke to him
from the crofs.——You go on, " But why fhould we believe
Peter, convicted by their own account of perjury, in
fwearing that he knew not Jefus?" I will tell you why—
becaufe Peter fincerely repented of the wickednefs into
which he had been betrayed through fear for his life, and
fuffered martyrdom in atteftation of the truth of the
Chriftian religion.

But the evangelifts difagree, you fay, not only as to the
fuperfcription on the crofs, but as to the time of the crucifixion, " Mark faying it was at the third hour (nine in the

morning,) and John at the fixth hour (twelve, as you
fuppofe, at noon)." Various folutions have been given
of this difficulty, none of which fatisfied Doctor Middleton,
much lefs can it be expected that any of them fhould fatisfy
you ; but there is a folution not noticed by him, in which
many judicious men have acquiefced—That John, writing
his gofpel in Afia, ufed the Roman method of computing
time ; which was the fame as our own : fo that by the fixth
hour, when Jefus was *condemned,* we are to underftand fix
o'clock in the morning ; the intermediate time from fix to
nine, when he was crucified, being employed in preparing
for the crucifixion. But if this difficulty fhould be ftill
efteemed infuperable, it does not follow that it will always
remain fo: and if it fhould, the main point, the crucifixion
of Jefus, will not be affected thereby.

I cannot, in this place, omit remarking fome circumftances attending the crucifixion, which are fo natural,
that we might have wondered if they had not occurred.
Of all the difciples of Jefus, John was beloved by him with
a peculiar degree of affection: and, as kindnefs produces
kindnefs, there can be little doubt that the regard was re-
ciprocal. Now whom fhould we expect to be the attendants
of Jefus in his laft fuffering? Whom but John the friend
of his heart?—Whom but his mother, whofe foul was now
pierced through by the fword of forrow, which *Simeon*
had foretold?—Whom but thofe, who had been attached
to him through life ; who, having been healed by him of
their infirmities, were impelled by gratitude to minifter to
him of their fubftance, to be attentive to all his wants?——
Thefe were the perfons whom we fhould have expected to
have attended his execution; and thefe were there. To
whom would an expiring fon, of the beft affections, recommend a poor, and, probably, a widowed mother,
but to his warmeft friend?—And this did Jefus.——Unmind-
ful of the extremity of his own torture, and anxious to
alleviate the burden of her forrows, and to protect her old
age from future want and mifery, he faid to his beloved
difciple——" Behold thy mother! and from that hour that
difciple took her to his own home." I own to you, that

such instances as these, of the conformity of events to our probable expectation, are to me genuine marks of the simplicity and truth of the gospels; and far outweigh a thousand little objections, arising from our ignorance of manners, times, and circumstances, or from our incapacity to comprehend the means used by the Supreme Being in the moral government of his creatures.

St. Matthew mentions several miracles which attended our Saviour's crucifixion——the darkness which overspread the land——the rending of the veil of the temple——an earthquake which rent the rocks—and the resurrection of many saints, and their going into the holy city——" Such," you say, " is the account which this dashing writer of the book of Matthew gives, but in which he is not supported by the writers of the other books." This is not accurately expressed; Matthew is supported by Mark and Luke, with respect to two of the miracles——the darkness——and the rending of the veil ; —and their omission of the others does not prove that they were either ignorant of them, or disbelieved them. I think it idle to pretend to say positively what influenced them to mention only two miracles ; they probably thought them sufficient to convince any person, as they convinced the centurion, that Jesus " was a righteous man"——" the Son of God." And these two miracles were better calculated to produce general conviction, amongst the persons for whose benefit Mark and Luke wrote their gospels, than either the earthquake or the resurrection of the saints. The earthquake was, probably confined to a particular spot, and might, by an objector, have been called a natural phenomenon ; and those to whom the saints appeared might, at the time of writing the gospels of Mark and Luke, have been dead ; but the darkness must have been generally known and remembered; and the veil of the temple might still be preserved at the time these authors wrote.——As to John not mentioning any of these miracles—it is well known that his gospel was written as a kind of supplement to the other gospels; he has therefore omitted many things which the other three evangelists had related, and he has added seve-

ral things which they had not mentioned; in particular,
he has added a circumstance of great importance: he tells
us that he saw one of the soldiers pierce the side of Jesus
with a spear, and that blood and water flowed through the
wound; and lest any one should doubt of the fact, from
its not being mentioned by the other evangelists, he asserts
it with peculiar earnestness——" And he that saw it, bare
record, and his record is true; and he knoweth that he
saith true, that ye might believe."——John saw blood and
water flowing from the wound; the blood is easily accounted for; but whence came the water? The anatomists
tell us——that it came from the *pericardium ;*——so con-
sistent is evangelical testimony with the most curious
researches into natural science!——You amuse yourself
with the account of what the Scripture calls *many* saints,
and you call an *army* of saints, and are angry with
Matthew for not having told you a great many things
about them.——It is very possible that Matthew might have
known the fact of their resurrection, without knowing
every thing about them; but if he had gratified your
curiosity in every particular, I am of opinion that you
would not have believed a word of what he had told you.
I have no curiosity on the subject; it is enough for me to
know that " Christ was the first-fruits of them that slept,"
and " that all that are in the graves shall hear his voice and
shall come forth," as those holy men did, who heard the
voice of the Son of God at his resurrection, and passed
from death to life. If I durst indulge myself in being wise
above what is written, I might be able to answer many
of your inquiries relative to these saints; but I dare not
touch the ark of the Lord, I dare not support the authority of Scripture by the boldness of conjecture. Whatever
difficulty there may be in accounting for the silence of the
other evangelists, and of St. Paul also, on this subject, yet
there is a greater difficulty in supposing that Matthew did
not give a true narration of what had happened at the
crucifixion. If there had been no supernatural darkness,
no earthquake, no rending of the veil of the temple, no
graves opened, no resurrection of holy men, no appearance

of them unto many—if none of these things had been true, or rather if any one of them had been false, what motive could Matthew, writing to the Jews, have had for trumping up such wonderful stories? He wrote, as every man does, with an intention to be believed; and yet every Jew he met would have stared him in the face, and told him that he was a liar and an impostor. What author, who twenty years hence should address to the French nation an history of Louis XVI. would venture to affirm, that when he was beheaded there was darkness for three hours over all France? that there was an earthquake? that rocks were split? graves opened? and dead men brought to life, who appeared to many persons in Paris?—It is quite impossible to suppose, that any one would dare to publish such obvious lies; and I think it equally impossible to suppose, that Matthew would have dared to publish his account of what happened at the death of Jesus, had not that account been generally known to be true.

LETTER VIII.

T HE "tale of the resurrection," you say, "follows that of the crucifixion."——You have accustomed me so much to this kind of language, that when I find you speaking of a tale, I have no doubt of meeting with a truth. From the apparent disagreement in the accounts, which the evangelists have given of some circumstances respecting the resurrection, you remark——" If the writers of these books had gone into any court of justice to prove an *alibi*, (for it is of the nature of an *alibi* that is here attempted to be proved, namely, the absence of a dead body by supernatural means,) and had given their evidence in the same contradictory manner, as it is here given, they would have been in danger of having their ears cropt for perjury, and would have justly deserved it"——" hard words, or

hanging," it feems, if you had been their judge. Now
I maintain, that it is the brevity with which the account
of the refurrection is given by all the evangelifts, which
has occafioned the feeming confufion; and that this confufion would have been cleared up at once, if the witneffes of the refurrection had been examined before any
judicature. As we cannot have this *viva voce* examination
of all the witneffes, let us call-up and queftion the evangelifts as witneffes to a fupernatural alibi.——Did you find
the fepulchre of Jefus empty? One of us actually faw
it empty, and the reft heard from eye-witneffes, that it
was empty.——Did you, or any of the followers of Jefus,
take away the dead body from the fepulchre? All anfwer, No.——Did the foldiers, or the Jews, take away
the body? No.——How are you certain of that? Becaufe
we faw the body when it was dead, and we faw it
afterwards when it was alive.—How do you know that
what you faw was the body of Jefus? We had been
long and intimately acquainted with Jefus, and knew his
perfon perfectly.——Were you not affrighted, and miftook
a fpirit for a body? No: the body had flefh and bones;
we are fure that it was the very body which hung upon
the crofs, for we faw the wound in the fide, and the
print of the nails in the hands and feet.——And all this you
are ready to fwear? We are; and we are ready to die
alfo, fooner than we will deny any part of it.——This is
the teftimony which all the evangelifts would give, in
whatever court of juftice they were examined; and this,
I apprehend, would fufficiently eftablifh the alibi of the
dead body from the fepulchre by fupernatural means.

But as the refurrection of Jefus is a point which you
attack with all your force, I will examine minutely the
principal of your objections; I do not think them de-
ferving of this notice, but they fhall have it. The book of
Matthew, you fay, " ftates that when Chrift was put in
the fepulchre, the Jews applied to Pilate for a watch or
a guard to be placed over the fepulchre, to prevent the
body being ftolen by the difciples."—I admit this account,
but it is not the whole of the account: you have omitted

the reafon for the requeft which the chief priefts made
to Pilate—" Sir, we remember that that deceiver faid, while
he was yet alive, After three days I will rife again."— It
is material to remark this; for at the very time that Jefus
predicted his refurrection, he predicted alfo his crucifixion,
and all that he fhould fuffer from the malice of thofe very
men who now applied to Pilate for a guard.——" He
fhewed to his difciples, how that he muft go unto Jerufalem, and fuffer many things of the elders, and chief
priefts, and fcribes, and be killed, and be raifed again the
third day." (Matt. xvi. 21.) Thefe men knew full well
that the firft part of this prediction had been accurately
fulfilled through their malignity; and, inftead of repenting
of what they had done, they were fo infatuated as to
fuppofe, that by a guard of foldiers they could prevent the
completion of the fecond.——" The other books," you
obferve, " fay nothing about this application, nor about
the fealing of the ftone, nor the guard, nor the watch, and
according to thefe accounts there were none."——This, Sir,
I deny. The other books do not fay that there were none
of thefe things; how often muft I repeat, that omiffions
are not contradictions, nor filence concerning a fact a
denial of it?

You go on——" The book of Matthew continues its
account, that at the end of the fabbath, as it began to
dawn, towards the firft day of the week, came *Mary Magdalene* and the other *Mary* to fee the fepulchre. Mark fays
it was fun-rifing, and John fays it was dark. Luke fays,
it was Mary Magdalene, and Joanna, and *Mary the mother
of James*, and *other women*, that came to the fepulchre;
and John fays that Mary Magdalene came alone. So well
do they agree about their firft evidence! they all appear,
however, to have known moft about Mary Magdalene;
fhe was a woman of a large acquaintance, and it was not
an ill conjecture that fhe might be upon the ftroll."—
This is a long paragraph; I will anfwer it diftinctly:——
firft, there is no difagreement of evidence with refpect to
the time when the women went to the fepulchre; all the
evangelifts agree as to the day on which they went; and,

as to the time of the day, it was early in the morning; what
court of juftice in the world would fet afide this evidence,
as infufficient to fubftantiate the fact of the women's
having gone to the fepulchre, becaufe the witneffes differ-
ed as to the degree of twilight which lighted them on
their way? Secondly, there is no difagreement of evidence with refpect to the perfons who went to the fepulchre. John ftates that Mary Magdalene went to the
fepulchre; but he does not ftate, *as you make him ftate*,
that Mary Magdalene went alone; fhe might, for any
thing you have proved, or can prove, to the contrary, have
been accompanied by all the women mentioned by Luke:
—is it an unufual thing to diftinguifh by name a principal
perfon going on a vifit, or an embaffy, without mentioning
his fubordinate attendants? Thirdly, in oppofition to
your infinuation that Mary Magdalene was a common
woman, I wifh it to be confidered, whether there is any
fcriptural authority for that imputation; and whether
there be or not, I muft contend, that a repentant and re-
formed woman ought not to be efteemed an improper
witnefs of a fact. The conjecture, which you adopt
concerning her, is nothing lefs than an illiberal, indecent,
unfounded calumny, not excufable in the mouth of a
libertine, and intolerable in yours.

The book of Matthew, you obferve, goes on to fay——
" And behold there was an earthquake, for the angel of the
Lord defcended from heaven, and came and rolled back
the ftone from the door, and *fat upon it*,——but the other
books fay nothing about any earthquake,"——what then?
does their filence prove that there was none?——" nor about
the angel rolling back the ftone and fitting upon it;"——
what then? does their filence prove that the ftone was not
rolled back by an angel, and that he did not fit upon it?——
" and according to their accounts, there was no angel fitting
there." This conclufion I muft deny; their accounts do
not fay there was no angel fitting there, at the time that
Matthew fays he fat upon the ftone. They do not deny
the fact, they fimply omit the mention of it; and they all
take notice that the women, when they arrived at the fe-

pulchre, found the ftone rolled away: hence it is evident that the ftone was rolled away *before* the women arrived at the fepulchre; and the other evangelifts, giving an account of what happened to the women *when* they reached the fepulchre, have merely omitted giving an account of a tranfaction previous to their arrival. Where is the contradiction? What fpace of time intervened between the rolling away the ftone, and the arrival of the women at the fepulchre, is no where mentioned; but it certainly was long enough for the angel to have changed his pofition; from fitting on the outfide he might have entered into the fepulchre; and another angel might have made his appearance; or, from the firft, there might have been two, one on the outfide rolling away the ftone, and the other within. " Luke," you tell us, " fays there were two, and they were both ftanding; and John fays there were two, and both fitting." —It is impoffible, I grant, even for an angel to be fitting and ftanding at the fame inftant of time; but Luke and John do not fpeak of the fame inftant, nor of the fame appearance—Luke fpeaks of the appearance to all the women; and John of the appearance to Mary Magdalene alone, who tarried weeping at the fepulchre after Peter and John had left it. But I forbear making any more minute remarks on ftill minuter objections, all of which are grounded on this miftake—that the angels were feen at one particular time, in one particular place, and by the fame individuals.

As to your inference, from Matthew's ufing the expreffion *unto this day*, " that the book muft have been manufactured after a lapfe of fome generations at leaft," it cannot be admitted againft the pofitive teftimony of all antiquity. That the ftory about ftealing away the body was a bungling ftory, I readily admit; but the chief priefts are anfwerable for it; it is not worthy either your notice or mine, except as it is a ftrong inftance to you, to me, and to every body how far prejudice may miflead the underftanding.

You come to that part of the evidence in thofe books that refpects, you fay, " the pretended appearances of Chrift after his pretended refurrection; the writer of the

book of Matthew relates, that the angel that was fitting
on the ftone at the mouth of the fepulchre faid to the two
Marys, (chap. xxviii. 7.) " Behold, Chrift is gone before
you into Galilee, there fhall you fee him." The gofpel,
Sir, was preached to poor and illiterate men : and it is the
duty of priefts to preach it to them in all its purity ; to
guard them againft the errors of miftaken, or the defigns
of wicked men. You then, who can read your Bible,
turn to this paffage, and you will find that the angel did
not fay, " Behold, Chrift *is gone* before you into Galilee,"
—but, " Behold, *he goeth* before you into Galilee." I
know not what Bible you made ufe of in this quotation,
none that I have feen render the original word by——he is
gone :——it might be properly rendered, he will go ; and
it is literally rendered, he is going. This phrafe does not im-
ply any immediate fetting out for Galilee : when a man has
fixed upon a long journey to London or Bath, it is common
enough to fay, he is going to London or Bath, though the
time of his going may be at fome diftance. Even your dafhing
Matthew could not be guilty of fuch a blunder as to make
the angel fay *he is gone ;* for he tells us immediately afterwards, that as the women were departing from the
fepulchre to tell his difciples what the angels had faid to
them, Jefus himfelf met them. Now how Jefus could be
gone into Galilee, and yet meet the women at Jerufalem,
I leave you to explain, for the blunder is not chargeable
upon Matthew. I excufe your introducing the expreffion
—" then the eleven difciples went away into Galilee," for
the quotation is rightly made ; but had you turned to the
Greek Teftament, you would not have found in this place
any word anfwering to *then ;* the paffage is better tranflated
—and the eleven. Chrift had faid to his difciples, (Matt.
xxvi. 32.) " After I am rifen again, I will go before you
into Galilee :"—and the angel put the women in mind of
the very expreffion and prediction—*He is rifen, as he faid ;
and behold, he goeth before you into Galilee.* Matthew, intent
upon the appearance in Galilee, of which there were,
probably, at the time he wrote, many living witneffes in
Judea, omits the mention of many appearances taken notice

of by John, and, by this omiffion, feems to connect the
day of the refurrection of Jefus, with that of the departure
of the difciples for Galilee. You feem to think this a great
difficulty, and incapable of folution; for you fay—"It is
not poffible, unlefs we admit thefe difciples the right of
wilful lying, that the writers of thefe books could be any
of the eleven perfons called difciples; for if, according to
Matthew, the eleven went into Galilee to meet Jefus in
a mountain, by his own appointment, on the fame day
that he is faid to have rifen, Luke and John muft have
been two of that eleven; yet the writer of Luke fays exprefsly and John implies as much, that the meeting was
that fame day in a houfe at Jerufalem: and on the other
hand, if, according to Luke and John, the *eleven* were
affembled in a houfe at Jerufalem, Matthew muft have been
one of that eleven; yet Matthew fays, the meeting was in a
mountain in Galilee; and confequently the evidence given
in thofe books deftroys each other." When I was a young
man in the univerfity, I was pretty much accuftomed to
drawing of confequences; but my *Alma Mater* did not
fuffer me to draw confequences after your manner; fhe
taught me—that a falfe pofition muft end in an abfurd
conclufion. I have fhewn your pofition—that the eleven
went into Galilee on the day of the refurrection—to be
falfe, and hence your confequence—that the evidence given
in thofe two books deftroys each other—is not to be admitted. You ought, moreover, to have confidered, that the
feaft of unleavened bread, which immediately followed the
day on which the paffover was eaten, lafted feven days;
and that ftrict obfervers of the law did not think themfelves
at liberty to leave Jerufalem, till that feaft was ended; and
this is a collateral proof that the difciples did not go to
Galilee on the day of the refurrection.

You certainly have read the New Teftament, but not,
I think, with great attention, or you would have known
who the Apoftles were. In this place you reckon *Luke* as
one of the eleven, and in other places you fpeak of him as
an eye-witnefs of the things he relates; you ought to have
known that Luke was no apoftle; and he tells you him-

felf, in the preface to his gofpel, that he wrote from the
teftimony of others. If this miftake proceeds from your
ignorance, you are not a fit perfon to write comments on
theBible; if from defign, (which I am unwilling to fufpect,)
you are ftill lefs fit; in either cafe it may fuggeft to your
readers the propriety of fufpecting the truth and accuracy
of your affertions, however daring and intemperate.—
" Of the numerous priefts or parfons of the prefent day,
bifhops and all, the fum total of whofe learning," according to you, " is a b ab, and hic, hæc, hoc, there is not one
amongft them," you fay, "who can write poetry like
Homer, or fcience like Euclid."—If I fhould admit this,
(though there are many of them, I doubt not, who underftand thefe authors better than you do,) yet I cannot admit that there is one amongft them, bifhops and all, fo
ignorant as to rank Luke the evangelift among the apoftles
of Chrift. I will not prefs this point ; any man may fall into
a miftake, and the confcioufnefs of this fallibility fhould
create in all men a little modefty, a little diffidence, a little
caution, before they prefume to call the moft illuftrious
characters of antiquity liars, fools, and knaves.

You want to know why Jefus did not fhew himfelf to
all the people after his refurrection.——This is one of Spinoza's objections ; and it may found well enough in the
mouth of a Jew, wifhing to excufe the infidelity of his
countrymen; but it is not judicioufly adopted by deifts of
other nations. God gives us the means of health, but he
does not force us to the ufe of them; he gives us the
powers of the mind, but he does not compel us to the
cultivation of them : he gave the Jews opportunities of
feeing the miracles of Jefus, but he did not oblige them to
believe them. They who perfevered in their incredulity
after the refurrection of Lazarus, would have perfevered
alfo after the refurrection of Jefus. Lazarus had been
buried four days, Jefus but three ; the body of Lazarus
had begun to undergo corruption, the body of Jefus faw
no corruption ; why fhould you expect, that they would
have believed in Jefus on his own refurrection, when they
had not believed in him on the refurrection of Lazarus ?

When the Pharifees were told of the refurrection of Lazarus, they, together with the chief priefts, gathered a council, and faid——" What do we? for this man doeth many
miracles. If we let him thus alone, all men will believe
on him; — then from that day forth they took counfel
together to put him to death." The great men at Jerufalem, you fee, admitted that Jefus had raifed Lazarus
from the dead; yet the belief of that miracle did not ge-
nerate conviction that Jefus was the Chrift; it only exas-
perated their malice, and accelerated their purpofe of
deftroying him. Had Jefus fhewn himfelf after his refurrection, the chief priefts would probably have gathered
another council, have opened it with, What do we? and
ended it with a determination to put him to death. As
to us, the evidence of the refurrection of Jefus, which we
have in the New Teftament, is far more convincing, than
if it had been related that he fhewed himfelf to every
man in Jerufalem; for then we fhould have had a fufpicion, that the whole ftory had been fabricated by the
Jews.

You think Paul an improper witnefs of the refurrection; I think him one of the fitteft that could have been
chofen; and for this reafon—his teftimony is the teftimony
of a former enemy. He had, in his own miraculous converfion, fufficient ground for changing his opinion as to a
matter of fact; for believing that to have been a fact,
which he had formerly, through extreme prejudice, confidered as a fable. For the truth of the refurrection of
Jefus, he appeals to above two hundred and fifty living
witneffes; and before whom does he make this appeal?
—Before his enemies, who were able and willing to blaft
his character, if he had advanced an untruth.——You know,
undoubtedly, that Paul had refided at Corinth near two
years; that, during a part of that time, he had teftified to
the Jews, that Jefus was the Chrift; that, finding the bulk
of that nation obftinate in their unbelief, he had turned to
the gentiles, and had converted many to the faith in
Chrift; that he left Corinth, and went to preach the gofpel in other parts; that, about three years after he had

quitted Corinth, he wrote a letter to the converts which he had made in that place, and who, after his departure, had been fplit into different factions, and had adopted different teachers in oppofition to Paul. From this account we may be certain, that Paul's letter, and every circumftance in it, would be minutely examined. The city of Corinth was full of Jews; thefe men were, in general, Paul's bitter enemies; yet, in the face of them all, he afferts, " that Jefus Chrift was buried; that he rofe again the third day; that he was feen of Cephas, then of the twelve; that he was afterwards feen of above five hundred brethren at once, of whom the greater part were then alive. An appeal to above two hundred and fifty living witneffes, is a pretty ftrong proof of a fact; but it becomes irrefiftible, when that appeal is fubmitted to the judgment of enemies. St. Paul, you muft allow, was a man of ability; but he would have been an idiot, had he put it in the power of his enemies to prove, from his own letter, that he was a lying rafcal. They neither proved, nor attempted to prove, any fuch thing, and therefore we may fafely conclude, that this teftimony of Paul to the refurrection of Jefus was true: and it is a teftimony, in my opinion, of the greateft weight.

You come, you fay, to the laft fcene, the afcenfion; upon which, in your opinion, " the reality of the future miffion of the difciples was to reft for proof."——I do not agree with you in this. The reality of the future miffion of the apoftles might have been proved, though Jefus Chrift had not vifibly afcended into heaven. Miracles are the proper proofs of a divine miffion; and when Jefus gave the apoftles a commiffion to preach the gofpel, he commanded them to ftay at Jerufalem, till they " were endued with power from on high." Matthew has omitted the mention of the afcenfion; and John, you fay, has not faid a fyllable about it. I think otherwife. John has not given an exprefs account of the afcenfion, but has certainly faid fomething about it; for he informs us, that Jefus faid to Mary——" Touch me not, for I am not yet *afcended* to my Father: but go to my brethren, and fay unto them,

I *afcend* unto my Father and your Father, and to my God and your God." This is furely faying fomething about the afcenfion: and if the fact of the afcenfion be not related by John or Matthew, it may reafonably be fuppofed, that the omiffion was made, on account of the notoriety of the fact. That the fact was generally known, may be juftly collected from the reference which Peter makes to it in the hearing of all the Jews, a very few days after it had happened——" This Jefus hath God raifed up, whereof we are all witneffes. Therefore being *by the right hand of God* exalted."——Paul bears teftimony alfo to the afcenfion, when he fays, that Jefus was *received up into glory.* As to the difference you contend for, between the account of the afcenfion, as given by Mark and Luke, it does not exift, except in this, that Mark omits the particulars of Jefus going with his apoftles to Bethany, and bleffing them there, which are mentioned by Luke. But omiffions, I muft often put you in mind, are not contradictions.

You have now, you fay, " gone through the examination of the four books afcribed to Matthew, Mark, Luke, and John; and when it is confidered that the whole fpace of time, from the crucifixion to what is called the afcenfion, is but a few days, apparently not more than three or four, and that all the circumftances are reported to have happened near the fame fpot, Jerufalem, it is, I believe, impoffible to find, in any ftory upon record, fo many, and fuch glaring abfurdities, contradictions, and falfehoods, as are in thofe books."——What am I to fay to this? Am I to fay that, in writing this paragraph, you have forfeited your character as an honeft man? Or, admitting your honefty, am I to fay that you are grofsly ignorant of the fubject? Let the reader judge.——John fays, that Jefus appeared to his difciples at Jerufalem on the day of his refurrection, and that Thomas was not then with them.——The fame John fays, that after *eight days* he appeared to them again, when Thomas was with them.—Now, Sir, how *apparently three or four days* can be confiftent with *really eight days*, I leave you to make out. But this is not the whole of John's teftimony, either with refpect to *place* or *time*——for he fays——After thefe

things (after the two appearances to the difciples at Jerufalem, on the firft and on the eighth day after the refurrection) Jefus fhewed himfelf again to his difciples at the fea
of *Tiberias.* The fea of Tiberias, I perfume you know,
was in Galilee; and Galilee, you may know, was fixty or
feventy miles from Jerufalem; it muft have taken the difciples fome time, after the eighth day, to travel from Jerufalem into Galilee. What, in your own infulting language
to the priefts, what have you to anfwer, as to the *fame fpot
Jerufalem,* as to your apparently *three or four days?* —But
this is not all. Luke, in the beginning of the Acts, refers
to his gofpel, and fays——" Chrift fhewed himfelf alive after
his paffion, by many infallible proofs, being feen of the
apoftles forty days, and fpeaking of the things pertaining
to the kingdom of God:" inftead of *four,* you perceive
there were *forty* days between the crucifixion and the afcenfion. I need not, I truft, after this, trouble myfelf
about the falfehood and contradictions which you impute
to the evangelifts; your readers cannot but be upon their
guard, as to the credit due to your affertions, however bold
and improper. You will fuffer me to remark, that the evangelifts were plain men; who, convinced of the truth of
their narration, and confcious of their own integrity, have
related what they knew, with admirable fimplicity. They
feem to have faid to the Jews of their time, and to fay to
the Jews and unbelievers of all times——We have told you
the truth; and if you will not believe us, we have nothing
more to fay.——Had they been impoftors, they would have
written with more caution and art, have obviated every
cavil, and avoided every appearance of contradiction. This
they have not done; and this I confider as a proof of their
honefty and veracity.

John the Baptift had given his teftimony to the truth
of our Saviour's miffion in the moft unequivocal terms;
he afterwards fent two of his difciples to Jefus, to afk him
whether he was really the expected Meffiah or not. Matthew relates both thefe circumftances: had the writer of
the book of Matthew been an impoftor, would he have
invalidated John's teftimony, by bringing forward his real

or apparent doubt? Impoſſible! Matthew, having proved
the reſurrection of Jeſus, tells us, that the eleven diſciples
went away into Galilee into a mountain where Jeſus had
appointed them, and " when they ſaw him, they worſhipped
him : but ſome doubted."—Would an impoſtor in the very
laſt place where he mentions the reſurrection, and in the
concluſion of his book, have ſuggeſted ſuch a cavil to
unbelievers, as to ſay—ſome doubted? Impoſſible! The
evangeliſt has left us to collect the reaſon why ſome
doubted :—The diſciples ſaw Jeſus, at a diſtance, on the
mountain ; and ſome of them fell down and worſhipped
him ; whilſt others doubted whether the perſon they ſaw
was really Jeſus ; their doubt, however, could not have
laſted long, for in the very next verſe we are told, that
Jeſus came and ſpake unto them.

Great and laudable pains have been taken by many
learned men, to harmonize the ſeveral accounts given us
by the evangeliſts of the reſurrection. It does not ſeem to
me to be a matter of any great conſequence to Chriſtianity,
whether the accounts can, in every minute particular, be
harmonized or not; ſince there is no ſuch diſcordance in
them, as to render the fact of the reſurrection doubtful to
any impartial mind. If any man, in a court of juſtice,
ſhould give poſitive evidence of a fact ; and three others
ſhould afterwards be examined, and all of them ſhould
confirm the evidence of the firſt as to the fact, but ſhould
apparently differ from him and from each other, by being
more or leſs particular in their accounts of the circumſtances attending the fact ; ought we to doubt of the fact,
becauſe we could not harmonize the evidence reſpecting
the circumſtances relating to it ? The omiſſion of any one
circumſtance (ſuch as that of Mary Magdalene having gone
twice to the ſepulchre; or that of the angel having, after
he had rolled away the ſtone from the ſepulchre, entered
into the ſepulchre) may render an harmony impoſſible,
without having recourſe to ſuppoſition to ſupply the defect.
You deiſts laugh at all ſuch attempts, and call them prieſt-
craft. I think it better then, in arguing with you, to admit
that there may be (not granting, however, that there is)

an irreconcileable difference between the evangelifts in fome of their accounts refpecting the life of Jefus, or his refurrection. Be it fo; what then? Does this difference, admitting it to be real, deftroy the credibility of the gofpel hiftory in any of its effential points? Certainly, in my opinion, not. As I look upon this to be a general anfwer to moft of your deiftical objections, I profefs my fincerity, in faying, that I confider it as a true and fufficient anfwer; and I leave it to your confideration. I have, purpofely, in the whole of this difcuffion, been filent as to the infpiration of the evangelifts; well knowing that you would have rejected with fcorn any thing I could have faid on that point; but, in difputing with a deift, I do moft folemnly contend, that the chriftian religion is true, and worthy of all acceptation, whether the evangelifts were infpired or not.

Unbelievers, in general, wifh to conceal their fentiments; they have a decent refpect for public opinion; are cautious of affronting the religion of their country; fearful of undermining the foundations of civil fociety. Some few have been more daring, but lefs judicious; and have, without difguife, profeffed their unbelief. But you are the firft who ever fwore that he was an infidel, concluding your deiftical creed with——So help me God! I pray that God may help you: that he may, through the influence of his Holy Spirit, bring you to a right mind; convert you to the religion of his Son, whom, out of his abundant love to mankind, he fent into the world, that all who believe in him fhould not perifh, but have everlafting life.

You fwear, that you think the chriftian religion is not true. I give full credit to your oath; it is an oath in confirmation——of what?——of an opinion.——It proves the fincerity of your declaration of your opinion; but the opinion, notwithftanding the oath, may be either true or falfe. Permit me to produce to you an oath not confirming an opinion, but a fact: it is the oath of St. Paul, when he fwears to the Galatians, that, in what he told them of his miraculous converfion, he did not tell a lie: "Now the things which I write unto you, behold, before God, I lie not."——Do but give that credit to Paul which I give to

you, do but confider the difference between an opinion
and a fact, and I fhall not defpair of your becoming a
chriftian.

Deifm, you fay, confifts in a belief of one God, and
an imitation of his moral character, or the practice of
what is called virtue; and in this (as far as religion is concerned) you reft all your hopes.——There is nothing in deifm
but what is in chriftianity, but there is much in chriftianity
which is not in deifm. The chriftian has no doubt concerning a future ftate; every deift, from Plato to Thomas
Paine, is on this fubject overwhelmed with doubts infuperable by human reafon. The chriftian has no mifgivings as
to the pardon of penitent finners, through the interceffion
of a mediator; the deift is haraffed with apprehenfion left
the moral juftice of God fhould demand, with inexorable
rigour, punifhment for tranfgreffion. The chriftian has no
doubt concerning the lawfulnefs and the efficacy of prayer;
the deift is difturbed on this point by abftract confiderations
concerning the goodnefs of God, which wants not to be
intreated; concerning his forefight, which has no need of
our information; concerning his immutability, which cannot
be changed through our fupplication. The chriftian admits
the providence of God, and the liberty of human actions;
the deift is involved in great difficulties, when he undertakes
the proof of either. The chriftian has affurance that the
Spirit of God will help his infirmities; the deift does not
deny the poffibility that God may have accefs to the human
mind, but he has no ground to believe the fact of his
either enlightening the underftanding, influencing the will,
or purifying the heart.

LETTER IX.

" T<small>HOSE</small>," you fay, " who are not much acquainted
with ecclefiaftical hiftory, may fuppofe that the book called
the New Teftament has exifted ever fince the time of Je-

fus Chrift; but the fact is hiftorically otherwife: there was
no fuch book as the New Teftament till more than three
hundred years after the time that Chrift is faid to have
lived."—This paragraph is calculated to miflead common
readers: it is neceffary to unfold its meaning. The book,
called the New Teftament, confifts of twenty-feven different parts; concerning feven of thefe, viz. the Epiftles to
the Hebrews, that of James, the fecond of Peter, the
fecond of John, the third of John, that of Jude, and the
Revelation, there were at firft fome doubts; and the question, whether they fhould be received into the canon,
might be decided, as all queftions concerning *opinions*
muft be, by vote. With refpect to the other twenty parts,
thofe who are moft acquainted with ecclefiaftical hiftory
will tell you, as Du Pin does after Eufebius, that they
were owned as canonical, at all times, and by all Chriftians.
Whether the council of Laodicea was held before or after
that of Nice, is not a fettled point; all the books of the
New Teftament, except the Revelations, are enumerated
as canonical in the Conftitutions of that council; but it is
a great miftake to fuppofe, that the greateft part of the
books of the New Teftament were not in *general ufe*
amongft Chriftians, long before the council of Laodicea
was held. This is not merely my opinion on the fubject;
it is the opinion of one much better acquainted with
ecclefiaftical hiftory than I am, and probably, than you
are—*Mofheim.* " The opinions," fays this author, " or
rather the conjectures, of the learned concerning the time
when the books of the New Teftament were collected into
one volume, as alfo about the authors of that collection,
are extremely different. This important queftion is attended with great and almoft infuperable difficulties to us
in thefe latter times. It is however fufficient for us to
know, that, before the middle of the fecond century, the
greateft part of the books of the New Teftament were
read in every Chriftian fociety throughout the world, and
received as a divine rule of faith and manners. Hence it
appears, that thefe facred writings were carefully feparated

from several human compositions upon the same subject, either by some of the apostles themselves, who lived so long, or by their disciples and successors, who were spread abroad through all nations. We are well assured, that the *four gospels* were collected during the life of St. John, and that the three first received the approbation of this divine apostle. And why may we not suppose, that the other books of the New Testament were gathered together at the same time? What renders this highly probable is, that the most urgent necessity required its being done. For, not long after Christ's ascension into heaven, several histories of his life and doctrines, full of pious frauds, and fabulous wonders, were composed by persons, whose intentions, perhaps, were not bad, but whose writings discovered the greatest superstition and ignorance. Nor was this all: productions appeared, which were imposed on the world by fraudulent men as the writings of the holy apostles. These apocryphal and spurious writings must have produced a sad confusion, and rendered both the history and the doctrine of Christ uncertain, had not the rulers of the church used all possible care and diligence in separating the books that were truly apostolical and divine, from all that spurious trash, and conveying them down to posterity in one volume."

Did you ever read the apology for the Christians, which Justin Martyr presented to the emperor Antoninus Pius, to the senate, and people of Rome? I should sooner expect a falsity in a petition, which any body of persecuted men, imploring justice, should present to the king and parliament of Great Britain, than in this apology.—— Yet in this apology, which was presented not fifty years after the death of St. John, not only parts of *all the four gospels are quoted*, but it is expressly said, that on the day called Sunday, a portion of them was read in the public assemblies of the Christians. I forbear pursuing this mat-ter farther; else it might easily be shewn, that probably the gospels, and certainly some of St. Paul's epistles, were known to *Clement, Ignatius,* and *Polycarp,* contemporaries with the apostles. These men could not quote or refer to books which did not exift: and therefore, though you could make it out that the book called the New Teftament did not formally exift under that title, till three hundred and fifty years after Chrift; yet I hold it to be a certain fact, that all the books, of which it is compofed, were written, and moft of them received by all Chriftians, within a few years after his death.

You raife a difficulty relative to the time which intervened between the death and refurrection of Jefus, who had faid, that the Son of Man fhall be three days and three nights in the heart of the earth.——Are you ignorant then that the Jews ufed the phrafe three days and three nights to denote what we underftand by three days?—— It is faid in Genefis, chap. vii. 12. "The rain was upon the earth forty days and forty nights;" and this is equivalent to the expreffion, (ver. 17.) "And the flood was forty days upon the earth." Inftead then of faying three days and three nights, let us fimply fay——three days——and you will not object to Chrift's being three days——Friday, Saturday, and Sunday——in the heart of the earth. I do not fay that he was in the grave the whole of either Friday or Sunday; but an hundred inftances might be produced, from writers of all nations, in which a part of a day is fpoken of as the whole. Thus much for the defence of the hiftorical part of the New Teftament.

You have introduced an account of *Fauftus*, as denying the genuinenefs of the books of the New Teftament. Will you permit that great fcholar in facred literature, *Michaelis*, to tell you fomething about this Fauftus?—— "He was ignorant, as were moft of the African writers, of the Greek language, and acquainted with the New Teftament merely through the channel of the Latin tranflation: he was not only devoid of a fufficient fund of learning, but illiterate in the higheft degree. An argument which he brings againft the genuinenefs of the gofpel affords fufficient ground for this affertion; for he contends, that the gofpel of St. Matthew could not have been written by St. Matthew himfelf, becaufe he is always mentioned in the third perfon." You know who has

argued like Fauſtus, but I did not think myſelf authorized
on that account to call you illiterate in the higheſt degree;
but Michaelis makes a ſtill more ſevere concluſion concerning Fauſtus; and he extends his obſervation to every man
who argued like him—" A man capable of ſuch an argument muſt have been ignorant not only of the Greek
writers, the knowledge of which could not have been
expected from Fauſtus, but even of the Commentaries of
Cæſar. And were it thought improbable that ſo heavy a
charge could be laid with juſtice on the ſide of his knowledge, it would fall with double weight on the ſide of his
honeſty, and induce us to ſuppoſe, that, preferring the arts
of ſophiſtry to the plainneſs of truth, he maintained opinions which he believed to be falſe." (Marſh's Tranſl.)
Never more, I think, ſhall we hear of Moſes not being the
author of the Pentateuch, on account of its being written
in the third perſon.

Not being able to produce any argument to render
queſtionable either the genuineneſs or the authenticity of
St. Paul's Epiſtles, you tell us, that " it is a matter of no
great importance by whom they were written, ſince the
writer, whoever he was, attempts to prove his doctrine by
argument; he does not pretend to have been witneſs to
any of the ſcenes told of the reſurrection and aſcenſion;
and he declares that he had not believed them." That
Paul had ſo far refiſted the evidence which the apoſtles
had given of the reſurrection and aſcenſion of Jeſus, as to
be a perſecutor of the diſciples of Chriſt is certain; but
I do not remember the place where he declares that he
had not believed them. The high prieſt and the ſenate
of the children of Iſrael, did not deny the reality of the
miracles, which had been wrought by Peter and the apoſtles; they did not contradict their teſtimony concerning
the reſurrection and the aſcenſion; but whether they believed it or not, they were fired with indignation, and took
counſel to put the apoſtles to death: and this was alſo
the temper of Paul; whether he believed or did not believe
the ſtory of the reſurrection, he was exceedingly mad
againſt the ſaints. The writer of Paul's Epiſtles does not

attempt to prove his doctrine by argument; he in many places tells us that his doctrine was not taught him by man, or any invention of his own, which required the ingenuity of argument to prove it : " I certify you, brethren, that the gofpel, which was preached of me, is not after man. For I neither received it of man, neither was I taught it, but by the revelation of Jefus Chrift." Paul does not pretend to have been a witnefs of the ftory of the refurrection, but he does much more; he afferts, that he was himfelf a witnefs of the refurrection. After enumerating many appearances of Jefus to his difciples, Paul fays of himfelf, " Laft of all, he was feen of me alfo, as of one born out of due time." Whether you will admit Paul to have been a *true* witnefs or not, you cannot deny that he pretends to have been *a* witnefs of the refurrection.

The ftory of his being ftruck to the ground, as he was journeying to Damafcus, has nothing in it, you fay, miraculous or extraordinary : you reprefent him as ftruck by lightning.—It is fomewhat extraordinary for a man, who is ftruck by lightning, to have, at the very time, full poffeffion of his underftanding ; to hear a voice iffuing from the lightning, fpeaking to him in the Hebrew tongue, calling him by his name, and entering into converfation with him. His companions, you fay, appear not to have fuffered in the fame manner :——the greater the wonder. If it was a common ftorm of thunder and lightning which ftruck Paul and all his companions to the ground, it is fomewhat extraordinary that he alone fhould be hurt; and that, notwithftanding his being ftruck blind by lightning, he fhould in other refpects be fo little hurt, as to be immediately able to walk into the city of Damafcus. So difficult is it to oppofe truth by an hypothefis!——In the character of Paul you difcover a great deal of violence and fanaticifm ; and fuch men, you obferve, are never good moral evidences of any doctrine they preach.—Read, Sir, Lord *Lyttleton's* obfervations on the converfion and apoftlefhip of St. Paul ; and I think you will be convinced of the contrary. That elegant writer thus expreffes his opinion on this fubject——" Befides all the proofs of the

chriſtian religion, which may be drawn from the prophecies of the Old Teſtament, from the neceſſary connection
it has with the whole ſyſtem of the Jewiſh religion, from
the miracles of Chriſt, and from the evidence given of his
reſurrection by all the other apoſtles, I think the con-
verſion and apoſtleſhip of St. Paul alone, duly conſidered,
is, of itſelf, a demonſtration ſufficient to prove chriſtianity
to be a divine revelation." I hope this opinion will have
ſome weight with you; it is not the opinion of a lying
Bible-prophet, of a ſtupid evangeliſt, or of an a b ab prieſt,
—but of a learned layman, whoſe illuſtrious rank received
ſplendor from his talents.

You are diſpleaſed with St. Paul " for ſetting out to
prove the reſurrection of the *ſame* body."——You know,
I preſume, that the reſurrection of the ſame body is not,
by all, admitted to be a ſcriptural doctrine.—" In the
New Teſtament (wherein, I think, are contained all the
articles of the chriſtian faith) I find our Saviour and the
apoſtles to preach the *reſurrection of the dead*, and the *reſurrection from the dead*, in many places; but I do not
remember any place where the reſurrection of the ſame
body is ſo much as mentioned." This obſervation of
Mr. Locke I ſo far adopt, as to deny that you can produce any place in the writings of St. Paul, wherein he
ſets out to prove the reſurrection of the ſame body. I do
not queſtion the poſſibility of the reſurrection of the ſame
body, and I am not ignorant of the manner in which
ſome learned men have explained it; (ſomewhat after the
way of your vegetative ſpeck in the kernel of a peach;) but
as you are diſcrediting St. Paul's doctrine, you ought to
ſhew that what you attempt to diſcredit is the doctrine
of the apoſtle. As a matter of choice, you had rather
have a better body—you will have a better body,—" your
natural body will be raiſed a ſpiritual body, your corruptible will put on incorruption." You are ſo much out of
humour with your preſent body, that you inform us, every
animal in the creation excels us in ſomething. Now I had
always thought, that the ſingle circumſtance of our having
hands, and their having none, gave us an infinite ſuperi-

ority not only over infects, fifhes, fnails, and fpiders, (which you reprefent as excelling us in loco-motive powers,) but over all the animals of the creation; and enabled us, in the language of Cicero, defcribing the manifold utility of our hands, to make as it were a new nature of things. As to what you fay about the confcioufnefs of exiftence being the only conceivable idea of a future life——it proves nothing, either for or againft the refurrection of a body, or of the fame body; it does not inform us, whether to any or to what fubftance, material or immaterial, this confcioufnefs is annexed. I leave it, however, to others, who do not admit perfonal identity to confift in confcioufnefs, to difpute with you on this point, and willingly fubfcribe to the opinion of Mr. Locke, "that nothing but confcious-nefs can unite remote exiftencies into the fame perfon."

From a caterpillar's paffing into a torpid ftate refem-bling death, and afterwards appearing a fplendid butterfly, and from the (fuppofed) confcioufnefs of exiftence which the animal had in thefe different ftates, you afk, " Why muft I believe, that the refurrection of the fame body is neceffary to continue in me the confcioufnefs of exiftence hereafter?"——I do not dislike analogical reafoning, when applied to proper objects, and kept within due bounds: — But where is it faid in Scripture, that the refurrection of the fame body is neceffary to continue in you the confci-oufnefs of exiftence? Thofe who admit a confcious ftate of the foul between death and the refurrection, will contend, that the foul is the fubftance in which confcioufnefs is con-tinued without interruption:——thofe who deny the inter-mediate ftate of the foul as a ftate of confcioufnefs, will contend that confcioufnefs is not deftroyed by death, but fufpended by it, as it is fufpended during a found fleep; and that it may as eafily be reftored after death, as after fleep, during which the faculties of the foul are not extinct, but dormant. Thofe who think that the foul is nothing diftinct from the compages of the body, not a fubftance but a mere quality, will maintain, that the confcioufnefs appertaining to every individual perfon is not loft when the body is deftroyed; that it is known to God; and may, at the general refurrection, be annexed to any fyftem of matter he may think fit, or to that particular compages to which it belonged in this life.

In reading your book I have been frequently fhocked at the virulence of your zeal, at the indecorum of your abufe in applying vulgar and offenfive epithets to men who have been held, and who will long, I truft, continue to be holden, in high eftimation. I know that the fcar of calumny is feldom wholly effaced; it remains long after the wound is healed; and your abufe of holy men and holy things will be remembered, when your arguments againft them are refuted and forgotten. Mofes you term an arrogant coxcomb, a chief affaffin; Aaron, Jofhua, Samuel, David, monfters and impoftors; the Jewifh kings a parcel of rafcals; Jeremiah and the reft of the prophets, liars; and Paul a fool, for having written one of the fublimeft compofitions, and on the moft important fubject that ever occupied the mind of man——the leffon in our burial fervice; ——this leffon you call a doubtful jargon, as deftitute of meaning as the tolling of the bell at the funeral. Men of low condition! preffed down, as you often are, by calamities generally incident to human nature, and groaning under burdens of mifery peculiar to your condition, what thought you when you heard this leffon read at the funeral of your child, your parent, or your friend? Was it mere jargon to you, as deftitute of meaning as the tolling of a bell?——No.——You underftood from it, that you would not all fleep, but that you would all be changed in a moment at the laft trump; you underftood from it, that this corruptible muft put on incorruption, that this mortal muft put on immortality, and that death would be fwallowed up in victory; you underftood from it, that if (notwithftanding profane attempts to fubvert your faith) ye continue fteadfaft, unmoveable, always abounding in the work of the Lord, your labour will not be in vain.

You feem fond of difplaying your fkill in fcience and philofophy; you fpeak more than once of Euclid; and, in cenfuring St. Paul, you intimate to us, that when the apoftle fays——one ftar differeth from another ftar in glory

——he ought to have faid——in diftance.—— All men *fee* that
one ftar differeth from another ftar in glory or brightnefs ;
but few men *know* that their difference in brightnefs arifes
from their difference in diftance; and I beg leave to fay,
that even you, philofopher as you are, do not *know* it.
You make an affumption which you cannot prove——that
the ftars are *equal* in magnitude, and placed at *different*
diftances from the earth ;——but you cannot prove that they
are not *different* in magnitude, and placed at *equal* diftances,
though none of them may be fo near to the earth, as to
have any fenfible annual *parallax.*——I beg pardon of my
readers for touching upon this fubject ; but it really moves
one's indignation, to fee a fmattering in philofophy urged
as an argument againft the veracity of an apoftle.——"Little
learning is a dangerous thing."

Paul, you fay, affects to be a naturalift ; and to prove
(you might more properly have faid illuftrate) his fyftem
of refurrection from the principles of vegetation——" Thou
fool," fays he, " that which thou foweft is not quickened
except it die ;"——to which one might reply, in his own
language, and fay——" Thou fool, Paul, that which thou
foweft is not quickened except it die *not.*" It may be
feen, I think, from this paffage, who affects to be a naturalift, to be acquainted with the microfcopical difcoveries
of modern times ; which were probably neither known to
Paul, nor to the Corinthians ; and which, had they been
known to them both, would have been of little ufe in the
illuftration of the fubject of the refurrection. Paul faid——
that which thou foweft is not quickened except it die :——
every hufbandman in Corinth, though unable perhaps to
define the term death, would underftand the apoftle's
phrafe in a popular fenfe, and agree with him that a grain
of wheat muft become *rotten* in the ground before it could
fprout : and that, as God raifed from a rotten grain of
wheat, the roots, the ftem, the leaves, the ear of a new
plant, he might alfo caufe a new body to fpring up from
the rotten carcafs in the grave.——Doctor *Clarke* obferves,
" In like manner as in every grain of corn there is contained a minute infenfible feminal principle, which is itfelf the

entire future blade and ear, and in due feafon, when all the
reft of the grain is corrupted, evolves and unfolds itfelf
vifibly to the eye; fo our prefent mortal and corruptible
body may be but the *exuviæ*, as it were, of fome hidden
and at prefent infenfible principle, (poffibly the prefent
feat of the foul,) which at the refurrection fhall difcover
itfelf in its proper form." I do not agree with this great
man (for fuch I efteem him) in this philofophical conjecture; but the quotation may ferve to fhew you, that the
germ does not evolve and unfold itfelf vifibly to the eye
till all the reft of the grain is *corrupted;* that is, in the language and meaning of St. Paul, till it *dies.*——Though the
authority of Jefus may have as little weight with you as
that of Paul, yet it may not be improper to quote to you
our Saviour's expreffion, when he foretells the numerous
difciples which his death would produce—" Except a corn
of wheat fall into the ground and *die,* it abideth alone;
but if it die, it bringeth forth much fruit."——You perceive
from this, that the Jews thought the death of the grain
was neceffary to its reproduction:—hence every one may
fee what little reafon you had to object to the apoftle's
popular illuftration of the poffibility of a refurrection.
Had he known as much as any naturalift in Europe does,
of the progrefs of an animal from one ftate to another, as
from a worm to a butterfly, (which you think applies to
the cafe,) I am of opinion he would not have ufed that
illuftration in preference to what he has ufed, which is
obvious and fatisfactory.

Whether the fourteen epiftles afcribed to Paul were
written by him or not, is, in your judgment, a matter of
indifference.——So far from being a matter of indifference,
I confider the genuinenefs of St. Paul's epiftles to be a
matter of the greateft importance: for if the epiftles,
afcribed to Paul, were written by him, (and there is un-
queftionable proof that they were,) it will be difficult for
you, or for any man, upon fair principles of found reafoning, to deny that the chriftian religion is true. The argument is a fhort one, and obvious to every capacity. It
ftands thus:——St. Paul wrote feveral letters to thofe whom,

in different countries, he had converted to the chriftian
faith; in thefe letters he affirms two things ;——firft, that he
had wrought miracles in their prefence;——fecondly, that
many of themfelves had received the gift of tongues, and
other miraculous gifts of the Holy Ghoft. The perfons to
whom thefe letters were addreffed, muft, on reading them,
have certainly known, whether Paul affirmed what was
true, or told a plain lie; they muft have known, whether
they had feen him work miracles: they muft have been
confcious, whether they themfelves did or did not poffefs
any miraculous gifts.——Now can you, or can any man,
believe, for a moment, that Paul (a man certainly of great
abilities) would have written public letters, full of lies, and
which could not fail of being difcovered to be lies, as foon
as his letters were read ?——Paul could not be guilty of
falfehood in thefe two points, or in either of them; and if
either of them be true, the chriftian religion is true. Refer-
ences to thefe two points are frequent in St. Paul's epiftles:
I will mention only a few.   In his Epiftle to the Galatians,
he fays, (chap. iii. 2, 5.) " This only would I learn of you,
received ye the fpirit (gifts of the fpirit) by the works of
the law?——He miniftereth to you the fpirit, and worketh
miracles among you."——To the Theffalonians he fays,
(1 Theff. ch. i. 5.) "Our gofpel came not unto you in word
only, but alfo in power, and in the Holy Ghoft."——To the
Corinthians he thus expreffes himfelf: (1 Cor. ii. 4.) " My
preaching was not with enticing words of man's wifdom,
but in the demonftration of the fpirit and of power;"——
and he adds the reafon for his working miracles —" That
your faith fhould not ftand in the wifdom of men, but in
the power of God."——With what alacrity would the fac-
tion at Corinth, which oppofed the apoftle, have laid hold
of this and many fimilar declarations in the letter, had they
been able to have detected any falfehood in them ! There
is no need to multiply words on fo clear a point——the genuinenefs of Paul's Epiftles proves their authenticity, inde-
pendently of every other proof: for it is abfurd in the extreme to fuppofe him, under circumftances of obvious
detection, capable of advancing what was not true: and if

Paul's Epiftles be both genuine and authentic, the chriftian religion is true.——Think of this argument.

You clofe your obfervations in the following manner : ——" Should the Bible (meaning, as I have before remarked, the Old Teftament) and Teftament hereafter fall, it is not I that have been the occafion." You look, I think, upon your production with a parent's partial eye, when you fpeak of it in fuch a ftyle of felf-complacency. The Bible, Sir, has withftood the learning of *Porphyry*, and the power of *Julian*, to fay nothing of the manichean *Fauftus* ——it has refifted the genius of *Bolingbroke*, and the wit of *Voltaire*, to fay nothing of a numerous herd of inferior affailants——and it will not fall by your force. You have barbed anew the blunted arrows of former adverfaries ; you have feathered them with blafphemy and ridicule; dipped them in your deadlieft poifon ; aimed them with your utmoft fkill; fhot them againft the fhield of faith with your utmoft vigour; but, like the feeble javelin of aged *Priam*, they will fcarcely reach the mark, will fall to the ground without a ftroke.

LETTER X.

The remaining part of your work can hardly be made the fubject of animadverfion. It principally confifts of unfupported affertions, abufive appellations, illiberal farcafms, *ftrifes of words, profane babblings, and oppofitions of fcience falfely fo called.* I am hurt at being, in mere juftice to the fubject, under the neceffity of ufing fuch harfh language; and am fincerely forry that, from what caufe I know not, your mind has received a wrong bias in every point refpecting revealed religion. You are capable of better things ; for there is a philofophical fublimity in fome of your ideas, when you fpeak of the Supreme Being, as the creator of the univerfe. That you may not accufe me of difrepect,

K

in paffing over any part of your work without beftowing
proper attention upon it, I will wait upon you through
what you call your——conclufion.

You refer your reader to the former part of the Age
of Reafon : in which you have fpoken of what you efteem
three frauds——myftery, miracle, and prophecy.——I have
not at hand the book to which you refer, and know not
what you have faid on thefe fubjects ; they are fubjects of
great importance, and we, probably, fhould differ effentially in our opinion concerning them ; but I confefs, I am
not forry to be excufed from examining what you have
faid on thefe points. The fpecimen of your reafoning,
which is now before me, has taken from me every inclination to trouble either my reader, or myfelf, with any obfervations on your former book.

You admit the poffibility of God's revealing his will
to man : yet " the thing fo revealed," you fay, " is revelation to the perfon only to whom it is made ; his account
of it to another is not revelation."——This is true ; his
account is fimple teftimony. You add, " there is no poffible criterion to judge of the truth of what he fays."——
This I pofitively deny : and contend, that a real miracle,
performed in atteftation of a revealed truth, is a certain
criterion by which we may judge of the truth of that
atteftation. I am perfectly aware of the objections which
may be made to this pofition ; I have examined them with
care ; I acknowledge them to be of weight ; but I do not
fpeak unadvifedly, or as wifhing to dictate to other men,
when I fay, that I am perfuaded the pofition is true. So
thought Mofes, when, in the matter of Korah, he faid to
the Ifraelites——" If thefe men die the common death of all
men, then the Lord hath not fent me."——So thought Elijah, when he faid, " Lord God of Abraham, Ifaac, and of
Ifrael, let it be known this day, that thou art God in
Ifrael, and that I am thy fervant ;"——and the people, before
whom he fpake, were of the fame opinion ; for, when the
fire of the Lord fell and confumed the burnt facrifice, they
faid——" The Lord he is the God."——So thought our
Saviour, when he faid——" The works that I do in my

Father's name, they bear witnefs of me;" and, " If I do
not the works of my Father, believe me not." What reafon have we to believe Jefus fpeaking in the gofpel, and to
difbelieve Mahomet fpeaking in the Koran ? Both of them
lay claim to a divine commiffion ; and yet we receive the
words of the one as a revelation from God, and we reject
the words of the other as an impofture of man. The
reafon is evident; Jefus eftablifhed his pretenfions, not by
alledging any fecret communication with the Deity, but
by working numerous and indubitable miracles in the prefence of thoufands, and which the moft bitter and watchful
of his enemies could not difallow; but Mahomet wrought
no miracles at all.—Nor is a miracle the only criterion by
which we may judge of the truth of a revelation. If a
feries of prophets fhould, through a courfe of many centuries, predict the appearance of a certain perfon, whom
God would, at a particular time, fend into the world for
a particular end ; and at length a perfon fhould appear,
in whom all the prodictions were minutely accomplifhed :
fuch a completion of prophecy would be a criterion of the
truth of that revelation, which that perfon fhould deliver
to mankind. Or if a perfon fhould now fay, (as many
falfe prophets have faid, and are daily faying) that he had
a commiffion to declare the will of God ; and, as a proof
of his veracity, fhould predict——that, after his death, he
would rife from the dead on the third day;—the completion of fuch a prophecy would, I prefume, be a fufficient
criterion of the truth of what this man might have faid
concerning the will of God. " Now I tell you, (fays Jefus
to his difciples, concerning Judas, who was to betray him),
before it come, that when it is come to pafs ye may believe that I am he." In various parts of the gofpels our
Saviour, with the utmoft propriety, claims to be received
as the meffenger of God, not only from the miracles which
he wrought, but from the prophecies which were fulfilled
in his perfon, and from the predictions which he himfelf
delivered. Hence, inftead of there being no criterion by
which we may judge of the truth of the Chriftian revelation, there are clearly three. It is an eafy matter to ufe an

indecorous flippancy of language in fpeaking of the Chriftian religion, and with a fupercilious negligence to clafs Chrift and his apoftles amongft the impoftors who have figured in the world ; but it is not, I think, an eafy matter for any man, of good fenfe and found erudition, to make an impartial examination into any one of the three grounds of Chriftianity which I have here mentioned, and to reject it.

What is it, you afk, the Bible teaches ?—The prophet Micah fhall anfwer you : it teacheth us—" to do juftly, to love mercy, and to walk humbly with our God ;"—juftice, mercy, and piety, inftead of what you contend for —rapine, cruelty, and murder. What is it, you demand, the Teftament teaches us ? You anfwer your queftion—to believe that the Almighty committed debauchery with a woman.—Abfurd and impious affertion! No, Sir, no ; this profane doctrine, this miferable ftuff, this blafphemous perverfion of Scripture, is your doctrine, not that of the New Teftament. I will tell you the leffon which it teaches to infidels as well as to believers ; it is a leffon which phi-lofophy never taught, which wit cannot ridicule, nor fo-phiftry difprove : the leffon is this — " The dead fhall hear the voice of the Son of God, and they that hear fhall live : all that are in their graves fhall come forth ; they that have done good, unto the refurrection of life ; and they that have done evil, unto the refurrection of damna-tion."

The moral precepts of the gofpel are fo well fitted to promote the happinefs of mankind in this world, and to prepare human nature for the future enjoyment of that bleffednefs, of which, in our prefent ftate, we can form no conception, that I had no expectation they would have met with your difapprobation. You fay, however,—" As to the fcraps of morality that are irregularly and thinly fcat-tered in thofe books, they make no part of the pretended thing, revealed religion."—"Whatfoever ye would that men fhould do to you, do you even fo to them."—Is this a fcrap of morality ? Is it not rather the concentred effence of all ethics, the vigorous root from which every branch of moral duty towards each other may be derived? Duties, you know, are diftinguifhed by moralifts into duties of perfect and imperfect obligation; does the Bible teach you nothing, when it inftructs you, that this diftinction is done away? when it bids you " put on bowels of mercies, kind-nefs, humblenefs of mind, meeknefs, long-fuffering, for-bearing one another and forgiving one another, if any man have a quarrel againft any." Thefe, and precepts fuch as thefe, you will in vain look for in the codes of *Frederic*, or *Juftinian;* you cannot find them in our ftatute books; they were not taught, nor are they taught, in the fchools of heathen philofophy; or, if fome one or two of them fhould chance to be glanced at by a Plato, a Seneca, or a Cicero, they are not bound upon the confciences of man-kind by any fanction. It is in the gofpel, and in the gofpel alone, that we learn their importance; acts of benevolence and brotherly love may be to an unbeliever voluntary acts, to a chriftian they are indifpenfable duties.—Is a new com-mandment no part of revealed religion? "A new command-ment I give unto you, That ye love one another;" the law of chriftian benevolence is enjoined us by Chrift himfelf in the moft folemn manner, as the diftinguifhing badge of our being his difciples.

Two precepts you particularife as inconfiftent with the dignity and the nature of man——that of not refenting injuries, and that of loving enemies.——Who but yourfelf ever interpreted literally the proverbial phrafe——"If a man fmite thee on thy right cheek, turn to him the other alfo?" —Did Jefus himfelf turn the other cheek when the officer of the high prieft fmote him? It is evident, that a patient acquiefcence under flight perfonal injuries is here enjoined; and that a pronenefs to revenge, which inftigates men to favage acts of brutality, for every trifling offence, is for-bidden. As to loving enemies, it is explained, in another place, to mean, the doing them all the good in our power; "if thine enemy hunger, feed him; if he thirft, give him drink:" and what think you is more likely to preferve peace, and to promote kind affections amongft men, than the returning good for evil? Chriftianity does not order us to love in proportion to the injury—" it does not offer a premium for a crime,"—it orders us to let our benevolence extend alike to all, that we may emulate the benignity of God himſelf, who maketh " his ſun to riſe on the evil and on the good."

In the law of Moſes, retaliation for deliberate injuries had been ordained—an eye for an eye, a tooth for a tooth. —*Ariſtotle*, in his treatiſe of morals, ſays, that ſome thought retaliation of perſonal wrongs an equitable proceeding; *Rhadamanthus* is ſaid to have given it his ſanction; the decemviral laws allowed it; the common law of England did not forbid it; and it is ſaid to be ſtill the law of ſome countries, even in Chriſtendom: but the mild ſpirit of Chriſtianity abſolutely prohibits, not only the retaliation of injuries, but the indulgence of every reſentful propenſity.

"It has been," you affirm, "the ſcheme of the chriſtian church to hold man in ignorance of the Creator, as it is of government to hold him in ignorance of his rights."—I appeal to the plain ſenſe of any honeſt man to judge whether this repreſentation be true in either particular. When he attends the ſervice of the church, does he diſcover any deſign in the miniſter to keep him in ignorance of his Creator? Are not the public prayers in which he joins, the leſſons which are read to him, the ſermons which are preached to him, all calculated to impreſs upon his mind a ſtrong conviction of the mercy, juſtice, holineſs, power, and wiſdom of the one adorable God, bleſſed for ever? By theſe means which the chriſtian church hath provided for our inſtruction, I will venture to ſay, that the moſt unlearned congregation of chriſtians in Great Britain have more juſt and ſublime conceptions of the Creator, a more perfect knowledge of their duty towards him, and a ſtronger inducement to the practice of virtue, holineſs, and temperance, than all the philoſophers of all the heathen countries in the world ever had, or now have. If, indeed, your ſcheme ſhould take place, and men ſhould no longer believe their Bible, then would they ſoon become as ignorant of the Creator, as all the world was when God called Abraham from his kindred; and as all the world, which has had no communication with either Jews or Chriftians, now is. Then would they foon bow down to ftocks and ftones, kifs their hand (as they did in the time of Job, and as the poor African does now,) to *the moon walking in brightnefs, and deny the God that is above;* then would they worfhip Jupiter, Bacchus, and Venus, and emulate, in the tranfcendent flagitioufnefs of their lives, the impure morals of their gods.

What defign has government to keep men in ignorance of their rights? None whatever.——All wife ftatesmen are perfuaded, that the more men know of their rights, the better fubjects they will become. Subjects, not from neceffity but choice, are the firmeft friends of every government. The people of Great Britain are well acquainted with their natural and focial rights; they underftand them better than the people of any other country do; they know that they have a right to be free, not only from the capricious tyranny of any one man's will, but from the more afflicting defpotifm of republican factions; and it is this very knowledge which attaches them to the conftitution of their country. I have no fear that the people fhould know too much of their rights; my fear is that they fhould not know them in all their relations, and to their full extent. The government does not defire that men fhould remain in ignorance of their rights; but it both defires, and requires, that they fhould not difturb the public peace, under vain pretences; that they fhould make themfelves acquainted, not merely with the rights, but with the duties alfo of men in civil fociety. I am far from ridiculing (as fome have done) the rights of man; I have long ago underftood, that the poor as well as the rich, and that the rich as well as the poor, have by nature fome rights, which no human government can juftly take from them, without their tacit or exprefs confent; and fome alfo, which they themfelves have no power to furrender to any government. One of the principal rights of man, in a ftate either of nature or of fociety, is a right of property in the fruits of his induſtry, ingenuity, or good fortune.——Does government hold any man in ignorance of this right? So much the contrary, that the chief care of government is to declare, aſcertain, modify, and defend this right; nay, it gives right, where nature gives none; it protects the goods of an inteſtate; and it allows a man at his death, to diſpoſe of that property, which the law of nature would cauſe to revert into the common ſtock. Sincerely as I am attached to the liberties of mankind, I cannot but profeſs myſelf an utter enemy to that ſpurious philoſophy, that democratic inſanity, which would equalize all property, and level all diſtinctions in civil ſociety. Perſonal diſtinctions, ariſing from ſuperior probity, learning, eloquence, ſkill, courage, and from every other excellency of talents, are the very blood and nerves of the body politic; they animate the whole, and invigorate every part; without them, its bones would become reeds, and its marrow water; it would preſently ſink into a fetid, ſenſeleſs maſs of corruption.——Power may be uſed for private ends, and in oppoſition to the public good; rank may be improperly conferred, and inſolently ſuſtained; riches may be wickedly acquired, and vicïouſly applied: but as this is neither neceſſarily, nor generally the caſe, I cannot agree with thoſe who, in aſſerting the natural equality of men, ſpurn the inſtituted diſtinctions attending power, rank, and riches.——But I mean not to enter into any diſcuſſion on this ſubject, farther than to ſay, that your crimination of government appears to me to be wholly unfounded; and to expreſs my hope, that no one individual will be ſo far miſled by diſquiſitions on the rights of man, as to think that he has any right to do wrong, as to forget that other men have rights as well as he.

You are animated with proper ſentiments of piety, when you ſpeak of the ſtructure of the univerſe. No one, indeed, who conſiders it with attention, can fail of having his mind filled with the ſupremeſt veneration for its Author. Who can contemplate, without aſtoniſhment, the motion of a comet, running far beyond the orb of

Saturn, endeavouring to efcape into the pathlefs regions of unbounded fpace, yet feeling, at its utmoft diftance, the attractive influence of the fun, hearing, as it were, the voice of God arrefting its progrefs, and compelling it, after a lapfe of ages, to reiterate its ancient courfe?—— Who can comprehend the diftance of the ftars from the earth, and from each other?—It is fo great, that it mocks our conception; our very imagination is terrified, confounded, and loft, when we are told, that a ray of light, which moves at the rate of above ten millions of miles in a minute, will not, though emitted at this inftant from the brighteft ftar, reach the earth in lefs than fix years.—— We think this earth a great globe; and we fee the fad wickednefs, which individuals are often guilty of, in fcraping together a little of its dirt: we view, with ftill greater aftonifhment and horror, the mighty ruin which has, in all ages, been brought upon human kind, by the low ambition of contending powers, to acquire a temporary poffeffion of a little portion of its furface. But how does the whole of this globe fink, as it were, to nothing, when we confider that a million of earths will fcarcely equal the bulk of the fun; that all the ftars are funs; and that millions of funs conftitute, probably, but a minute portion of that material world, which God hath diftributed through the immenfity of fpace.——Syftems, however, of infenfible matter, though arranged in exquifite order, prove only the wifdom and the power of the great Architect of nature.——As percipient beings, we look for fomething more—for his goodnefs—and we cannot open our eyes without feeing it.

Every portion of the earth, fea, and air, is full of fenfitive beings, capable, in their refpective orders, of enjoying the good things which God has prepared for their comfort. All the orders of beings are enabled to propagate their kind; and thus provifion is made for a fucceffive continuation of happinefs. Individuals yield to the law of diffolution, infeparable from the material ftructure of their bodies: but no gap is thereby left in exiftence; their place is occupied by other individuals capable of participating in the goodnefs of the Almighty. Contem-

plations fuch as thefe fill the mind with humility, benevolence, and piety. But why fhould we ftop here? why
not contemplate the goodnefs of God in the redemption,
as well as in the creation of the world? By the death of
his only begotten Son Jefus Chrift, he hath redeemed the
whole human race from the eternal death, which the transgreffion of Adam had entailed on all his pofterity.——You
believe nothing about the tranfgreffion of Adam. The
hiftory of Eve and the ferpent excites your contempt; you
will not admit that it is either a real hiftory, or an alle-
gorical reprefentation of death entering into the world
through fin, through difobedience to the command of
God.——Be it fo.——You find, however, that death doth
reign over all mankind, by whatever means it was introduced: this is not a matter of belief, but of lamentable
knowledge.——The New Teftament tells us, that through
the merciful difpenfation of God, Chrift hath overcome
death, and reftored man to that immortality which Adam
had loft: this alfo you refufe to believe.——Why? Becaufe
you cannot account for the propriety of this redemption.
Miferable reafon! ftupid objection! What is there that
you can account for? Not for the germination of a blade
of grafs, not for the fall of a leaf of the foreft——and will
you refufe to eat of the fruits of the earth, becaufe God
has not given you wifdom equal to his own? Will you
refufe to lay hold on immortality, becaufe he has not
given you, becaufe he, probably, could not give to
fuch a being as man, a full manifeftation of the end
for which he defigns him, nor of the means requifite for
the attainment of that end? What father of a family can
make level to the apprehenfion of his infant children,
all the views of happinefs which his paternal goodnefs is
preparing for them? How can he explain to them the
utility of reproof, correction, inftruction, example, of all
the various means by which he forms their minds to piety,
temperance, and probity? We are children in the hand
of God: we are in the very infancy of our exiftence;
juft feparated from the womb of eternal duration; it
may not be poffible for the Father of the univerfe to explain to us (infants in apprehenfion!) the goodnefs and the

wifdom of his dealings with the fons of men. What qualities of mind will be neceffary for our well-doing through all eternity, we know not; what difcipline in this infancy of exiftence may be neceffary for generating thefe qualities, we know not: whether God could or could not, confiftently with the general good, have forgiven the transgreffion of Adam, without any atonement, we know not; whether the malignity of fin be not fo great, fo oppofite to the general good, that it cannot be forgiven whilft it exifts, that is, whilft the mind retains a propenfity to it, we know not: fo that, if there fhould be much greater difficulty in comprehending the mode of God's moral government of mankind, than there really is, there would be no reafon for doubting of its rectitude. If the whole human race be confidered as but one fmall member of a large community of free and intelligent beings of different orders, and if this whole community be fubject to difcipline and laws productive of the greateft poffible good to the whole fyftem, then may we ftill more reafonably fufpect our capacity to comprehend the wifdom and goodnefs of all God's proceedings in the moral government of the univerfe.

You are lavifh in your praife of deifm; it is fo much better than atheifm, that I mean not to fay any thing to its difcredit; it is not, however, without its difficulties. What think you of an uncaufed caufe of every thing? of a Being who has no relation to time, not being older to-day than he was yefterday, nor younger to-day than he will be to-morrow? who has no relation to fpace, not being a part here and a part there, or a whole any where? What think you of an omnifcient Being, who cannot know the future actions of a man? Or, if his omnifcience enables him to know them, what think you of the contingency of human actions? And if human actions are not contingent, what think you of the morality of actions, of the diftinction between vice and virtue, crime and innocence, fin and duty? What think you of the infinite goodnefs of a Being who exifted through eternity, without any emanation of his goodnefs manifefted in the creation of fenfitive beings? Or, if you contend that there has been an eternal creation,

what think you of an effect coeval with its caufe, of matter not pofterior to its Maker? What think you of the
exiftence of evil, moral and natural, in the work of an infinite Being, powerful, wife, and good? What think you of
the gift of freedom of will, when the abufe of freedom becomes the caufe of general mifery? I could propofe to your
confideration a great many other queftions of a fimilar
tendency, the contemplation of which has driven not a few
from deifm to atheifm, juft as the difficulties in revealed
religion have driven yourfelf, and fome others, from chris-
tianity to deifm.

For my own part, I can fee no reafon why either revealed or natural religion fhould be abandoned, on account
of the difficulties which attend either of them. I look up
to the incomprehenfible Maker of heaven and earth with
unfpeakable admiration and felf-annihilation, and am a
deift.——I contemplate, with the utmoft gratitude and humility of mind, his unfearchable wifdom and goodnefs in
the redemption of the world from eternal death, through
the intervention of his Son Jefus Chrift, and am a chriftian.
——As a deift, I have little expectation; as a chriftian, I
have no doubt of a future ftate. I fpeak for myfelf, and
may be in an error, as to the ground of the firft part of this
opinion. You and other men may conclude differently.
From the inert nature of matter—From the faculties of the
human mind—from the apparent imperfection of God's
moral government of the world——from many modes of
analogical reafoning, and from other fources, fome of the
philofophers of antiquity did collect, and modern philofophers may, perhaps, collect a ftrong probability of a future
exiftence; and not only of a future exiftence, but (which
is quite a diftinct queftion) of a future ftate of retribution,
proportioned to our moral conduct in this world. Far be
it from me to loofen any of the obligations to virtue; but
I muft confefs, that I cannot, from the fame fources of argumentation, derive any pofitive affurance on the fubject.
Think then with what thankfulnefs of heart I receive the
word of God, which tells me, that though " in Adam (by
the condition of our nature) all die;" yet " in Chrift (by
the covenant of grace) fhall all be made alive." I lay hold

on " eternal life as the gift of God through Jefus Chrift;"
I confider it not as any appendage to the nature I derive
from Adam, but as the free gift of the Almighty, through
his Son, whom he has conftituted Lord of all, the Saviour,
the Advocate, and the Judge of human kind.

" Deifm," you affirm, " teaches us, without the poffibility of being miftaken, all that is neceffary or proper to
be known."——There are three things, which all reafonable
men admit are neceffary and proper to be known——the
being of God——the providence of God——a future ftate of
retribution.——Whether thefe three truths are fo taught us
by deifm, that there is no poffibility of being miftaken concerning any of them, let the hiftory of philofophy, and of
idolatry and fuperftition, in all ages and countries, determine. A volume might be filled with an account of the
miftakes into which the greateft reafoners have fallen, and
of the uncertainty in which they lived, with refpect to
every one of thefe points. I will advert, briefly, only to
the laft of them. Notwithftanding the illuftrious labours of
Gaffendi, Cudworth, Clarke, Baxter, and of above two hundred other modern writers on the fubject, the *natural* mor-
tality or immortality of the human foul is as little underftood by us, as it was by the philofophers of Greece or
Rome. The oppofite opinions of *Plato* and of *Epicurus,*
on this fubject, have their feveral fupporters amongft the
learned of the prefent age, in Great Britain, Germany,
France, Italy, in every enlightened part of the world : and
they who have been moft ferioufly occupied in the ftudy
of the queftion concerning a future ftate, as deducible from
the nature of the human foul, are leaft difpofed to give
from reafon a pofitive decifion of it either way. The importance of revelation is by nothing rendered more apparent, than by the difcordant fentiments of learned and
good men (for I fpeak not of the ignorant and immoral) on
this point. They fhew the infufficiency of human reafon, in a courfe of above two thoufand years, to unfold
the myfteries of human nature, and to furnifh, from the
contemplation of it, any affurance from the quality of our
future condition. If you fhould ever become perfuaded

L

of this infufficiency, (and you can fcarce fail of becoming
fo, if you examine the matter deeply,) you will, if you act
rationally, be difpofed to inveftigate, with ferioufnefs and
impartiality, the truth of Chriftianity. You will fay of the
gofpel, as the *Northumbrian* heathens faid of *Paulinus*, by
whom they were converted to the Chriftian religion—
" The more we reflect on the nature of our foul, the lefs
we know of it. Whilft it animates our body, we may
know fome of its properties; but when once feparated,
we know not whither it goes, or from whence it came.
Since then the *gofpel* pretends to give us clearer notions of
thefe matters, we ought to hear it, and, laying afide all
paffion and prejudice, follow that which fhall appear moft
conformable to right reafon."

What a bleffing is it to beings, with fuch limited capa-
cities as ours confeffedly are, to have God himfelf for our
inftructor in every thing which it much concerns us to
know! We are principally concerned in knowing—not the
origin of arts, or the recondite depths of fcience—not the
hiftories of mighty empires defolating the globe by their
contentions—not the fubtilties of logic, the myfteries of
metaphyfics, the fublimities of poetry, or the niceties of
criticifm.—Thefe, and fubjects fuch as thefe, properly
occupy the learned leifure of a few; but the bulk of human kind have ever been, and muft ever remain, ignorant
of them all; they muft, of neceffity, remain in the fame
ftate with that which a German emperor voluntarily put
himfelf into, when he made a refolution, bordering on
barbarifm, that he would never read a printed book. We
are all, of every rank and condition, equally concerned in
knowing—what will become of us after death;—and, if
we are to live again, we are interefted in knowing—
whether it be poffible for us to do any thing whilft we live
here, which may render that future life an happy one.—
Now, " that thing called Chriftianity," as you fcoffingly
fpeak—that laft beft gift of Almighty God, as I efteem it,
the gofpel of Jefus Chrift, has given us the moft clear and
fatisfactory information on both thefe points. It tells us,
what deifm never could have told us, that we fhall certainly

be raifed from the dead——that, whatever be the nature of the foul, we fhall certainly live for ever—and that, whilft we live here, it is poffible for us to do much towards the rendering that everlafting life an happy one.——Thefe are tremendous truths to bad men; they cannot be received and reflected on with indifference by the beft; and they fuggeft to all fuch a cogent motive to virtuous action, as deifm could not furnifh even to *Brutus* himfelf.

Some men have been warped to infidelity by vicioufnefs of life; and fome may have hypocritically profeffed chriftianity from profpects of temporal advantage; but, being a ftranger to your character, I neither impute the former to you, nor can admit the latter as operating on myfelf. The generality of unbelievers are fuch, from want of information on the fubject of religion; having been engaged from their youth in ftruggling for worldly diftinction, or perplexed with the inceffant intricacies of bufinefs, or bewildered in the purfuits of pleafure, they have neither ability, inclination, nor leifure, to enter into critical difquifitions concerning the truth of chriftianity. Men of this defcription are foon ftartled by objections which they are not competent to anfwer: and the loofe morality of the age (fo oppofite to chriftian perfection!) co-operating with their want of fcriptural knowledge, they prefently get rid of their nurfery faith, and are feldom fedulous in the acquifition of another, founded, not on authority, but fober inveftigation. Prefuming, however, that many deifts are as fincere in their belief as I am in mine, and knowing that fome are more able, and all as much interefted as myfelf, to make a rational inquiry into the truth of revealed religion, I feel no propenfity to judge uncharitably of any of them. They do not think as I do, on a fubject furpaffing all others in importance; but they are not on that account, to be fpoken of by me with afperity of language, to be thought of by me as perfons alienated from the mercies of God. The gofpel has been offered to their acceptance; and from whatever caufe they reject it, I cannot but efteem their fituation to be dangerous. Under the influence of that perfuafion I have been induced to write this book. I do not expect to derive from it either fame or profit: thefe are not improper incentives to honourable activity; but there is a time of life when they ceafe to direct the judgment of thinking men. What I have written will not, I fear, make any impreffion on you; but I indulge an hope, that it may not be without its effect on fome of your readers. Infidelity is a rank weed, it threatens to overfpread the land; its root is principally fixed amongft the great and opulent; but you are endeavouring to extend the malignity of its poifon through all the claffes of the community. There is a clafs of men, for whom I have the greateft refpect, and whom I am anxious to preferve from the contamination of your irreligion—the merchants, manufacturers, and tradefmen of the kingdom. I confider the influence of the example of this clafs as effential to the welfare of the community. I know that they are in general given to reading, and defirous of information on all fubjects.

If this little book fhould chance to fall into their hands after they have read yours, and they fhould think that any of your objections to the authority of the Bible have not been fully anfwered, I intreat them to attribute the omiffion to the brevity which I have ftudied; to my defire of avoiding learned difquifitions; to my inadvertency; to my inability; to any thing, rather than to an impoffibility of completely obviating every difficulty you have brought forward. I addrefs the fame requeft to fuch of the youth of both fexes, as may unhappily have imbibed, from your writings, the poifon of infidelity; befeeching them to believe, that all their religious doubts may be removed, though it may not have been in my power to anfwer, to their fatisfaction, all your objections. I pray God that the rifing generation of this land may be preferved from that "evil heart of unbelief," which has brought ruin on a neighbouring nation; that neither a neglected education, nor domeftic irreligion, nor evil communication, nor the fafhion of a licentious world may ever induce them to forget, that religion alone ought to be their rule of life.

In the conclufion of my *Apology for Chriftianity*, I informed Mr. Gibbon of my extreme averfion to public controverfy. I am now twenty years older than I was then, and I perceive that this my averfion has increafed with my age. I have, through life, abandoned my little literary productions to their fate; fuch of them as have been attacked, have never received any defence from me; nor will this receive any, if it fhould meet with your public notice, or with that of any other man.

Sincerely wifhing that you may become a partaker of that faith in revealed religion, which is the foundation of my happinefs in this world, and of all my hopes in another, I bid you farewell.

R. LANDAFF.

Calgarth Park,
   Jan. 20, 1796.